The Hammers of
Towan

The
HAMMERS
of
TOWAN

A Nineteenth-Century Cornish Family

Sue Appleby

Matador
9 Priory Business Park,
Wistow Road, Kibworth Beauchamp,
Leicestershire. LE8 0RX
Tel: 0116 279 2299
Email: books@troubador.co.uk
Web: www.troubador.co.uk/matador
Twitter: @matadorbooks

ISBN 978 1800463 202

British Library Cataloguing in Publication Data.
A catalogue record for this book is available from the British Library.

Printed and bound by CPI Group (UK) Ltd, Croydon, CR0 4YY
Typeset in 12pt Adobe Jenson Pro by Troubador Publishing Ltd, Leicester, UK

Matador is an imprint of Troubador Publishing Ltd

For my mother, Dora Irene Marjorie Hammer – for passing on the stories, for keeping the photos and, most importantly, for identifying who was in those photos.

PHILIP HENRY AND JANE

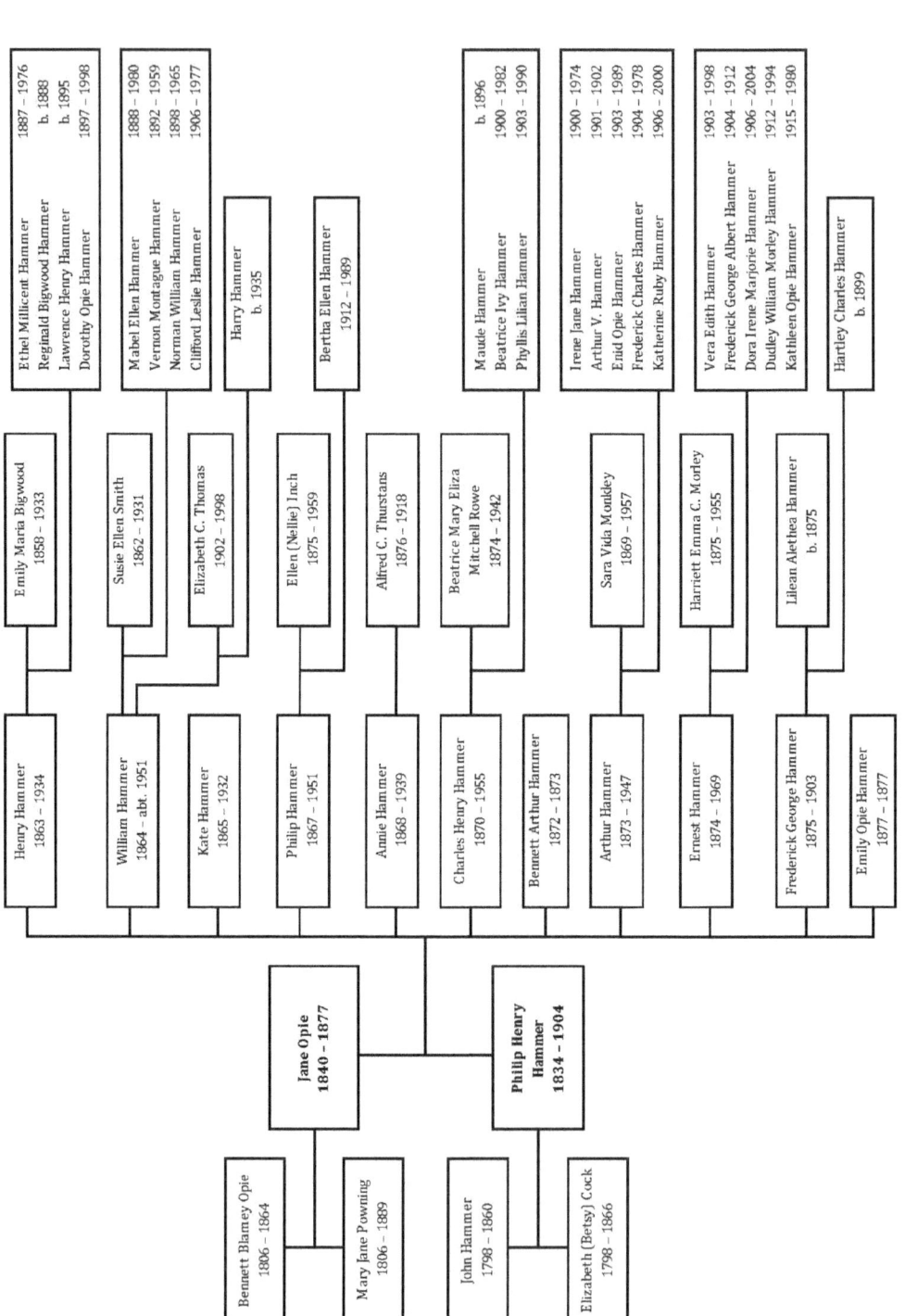

PHILIP HENRY AND REBECCA

PHILIP HENRY AND EMILY JANE

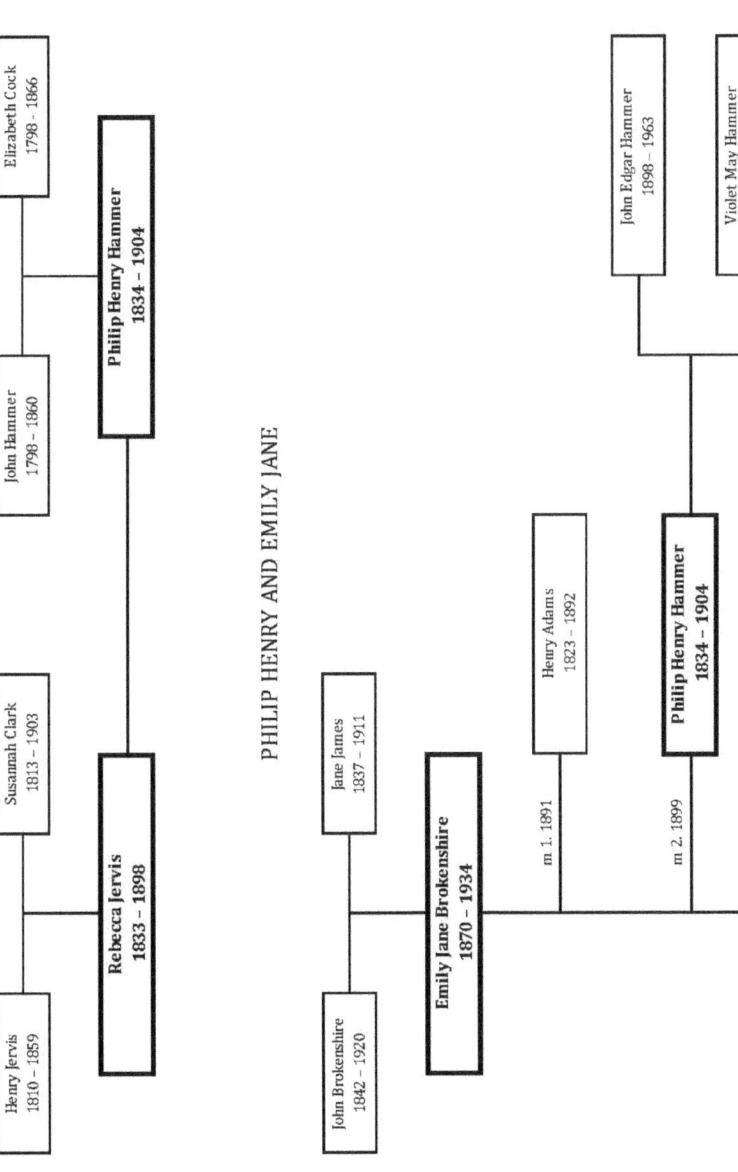

Contents

List of Illustrations

Table

Acknowledgements

Thank you to Dave and Enoch Pengelly for helping me to know more about Towan, to Mike and Averil Inglefield for their hospitality and for all the stories about Cornwall, to the Coomber family and to Margaret Blight and Violet Gold for cups of tea and conversations about the Hammer family. Also, to Robin Davies for helping to locate Charlestown Mill's cottage, and to Nan Goldsworthy for her endless supply of useful contacts, names, and phone numbers.

For help with my research I much appreciate the assistance given to me by Angela Broome at the Courtney Library, Royal Cornwall Museum; by Kim Cooper and the staff at the Cornish Studies Centre – now part of Kresen Kernow – and by the volunteers at the Cornwall Family History Society.

Many thanks to Philip Payton for taking the time to read my manuscript in search of historical errors, and to Deborah Eckert for her black-and-white line drawings which complement the text so perfectly.

A special thank you to my family: to my daughter Meiling for editing the old photographs, to husband Bernie for letting me disappear off to Cornwall for extended periods, and to daughter Sarah for keeping Bernie company while I was away from home. Other family members provided invaluable information and photos: Stephen Appleby, Sandra Burt, and Chris and Sue Starr.

In conclusion, many thanks to my copy-editors Helen and Adrian Stenton for their careful work, to John Evans for agreeing to publish my manuscript, to Rachel Hall for designing the cover, and to Duncan Evans for devoting his time to the publishing process.

Sue Appleby, Antigua, 2013

Acknowledgements – 2nd Edition

A few years have passed since I wrote *The Hammers of Towan*, but since the book's publication in 2013 – as sometimes happens when a writing project is supposedly finished – more important information has come to light, old Cornish recipes have been unearthed, more stories have been told and some lost photos have been found.

Thank you to Deborah Eckert for her illustration of Towan Holy Well, and to cousin Mike Chard – both for photos of the Hammer family that were new to me, and for long and fascinating conversations about the family. Daughter Meiling has done an excellent job of designing new diagrams for Philip Henry and Jane Opie and their nineteenth-century families.

It was a pleasure to meet Guy and Catherine English, and to learn about their ongoing research into the holy wells of Cornwall, which helped me to understand the importance of the well on Towan Farm. Andrew van Lingen provided me with invaluable information as I searched for details about the dynamite explosion which killed my great uncle in South Africa. And it is always good to exchange messages with Kathy Anstiss, as we both continue to research our family trees and fill in some of the missing pieces in the Hammer family history puzzle.

Old Cornish recipes make up an important part of this 2nd edition of *The Hammers of Towan*, and I must thank The Cornwall Federation of Women's Institutes for allowing me to quote in some detail from their 1929 publication compiled by Edith Martin: *Cornish Recipes Ancient and Modern*.

I again much appreciate the information resources provided by Angela Broome at the Courtney Library, Royal Cornwall Museum, and by the staff at Kresen Kernow and the Morrab Library. Carole Green from

Archives and Special Collections at Falmouth University, and members of the St Austell Old Cornwall Society also helped with my research.

Caroline Petherick, my copy editor, and Dan Coxon, my proof reader, both did an excellent job, while the expert team at Troubador Publishing guided me smoothly through the publishing process, from receipt of my manuscript to publication under their Matador imprint.

So, eight years after the publication of the first edition of *The Hammers of Towan*, here again – but in a much extended version – is their story.

Sue Appleby, Antigua, 2021

Introduction

I am of Cornish heritage on my mother's side of the family. Mother was born in London, but her father, Ernest Hammer, was born on the farm then known as Towan,[i] which lies near to Cornwall's southern coast, close to the villages of Porthpean[ii] and Pentewan, and not far from the port of Charlestown and the town of St Austell. Ernest left Cornwall as a young man and moved to Hackney in London, where he became a master butcher, but when he later bought a farm in Essex, he gave it a Cornish name – Pentowan – and when he built a house for his retirement, he called it St Austell. Here, in his garden – perhaps to again remind himself of where he came from – he planted a monkey puzzle tree and a large circular bed of pampas grass, both common in Cornwall but rarely seen in Essex. Several generations of his family, including my own, returned often to Cornwall, so I grew up with something of Cornwall woven into my life.

When I was a child, annual summer holidays were spent in and around Looe, Charlestown, Porthpean, Pentewan and Fowey.[iii] We would start out from our Essex farm in the family car in the middle of the night, to miss the worst of the traffic by the time we reached Exeter in Devon. I would fall asleep in the back of the car and wake up as dawn rose over Salisbury Plain and we passed the mysterious Stonehenge. 'Aren't we there *yet?*' I would always ask. Finally, leaving Devon behind, we crossed the River Tamar, and mother would say, 'Now we're in Cornwall.'

Days were spent on pebbly beaches poking around in tide pools, picking up stones that looked shiny and full of colour when wet but became flat, colourless and merely heavy when dry, taking home thick

---

i   Pronounced 'Town' but with the addition of a slight emphasis on the 'a'.
ii Rhymes with 'European'; and, as with most Cornish place names, the stress is on the second syllable.
iii Pronounced 'Foy'.

rubbery strands of seaweed and hanging them up on a nail: 'You can tell the weather by it,' mother said. 'When it's hard and crispy the weather will be fine and dry; when it's damp and soft we shall have rain.'

There was Cornish food: pasties were regular fare on the farm at home and often taken on picnics. Mother's standards were high: 'Short-crust pastry not too thick, and good steak cut up into pieces – none of this flaky pastry and minced meat, and please don't let me see you eat it with a knife and fork!' Big flat round pans of milk from our cows would be set over the pilot light on the gas stove overnight, and thick clotted cream would be there to be scooped off the next morning: so good on a thick slice of new crusty bread with golden syrup spread over it – but not so good when it was my job to make the cream into butter by turning and turning the handle of the butter churn in the dairy; would it ever become butter? Baking saffron cake when we could get the saffron, eating scones with strawberry jam and yet more clotted cream for tea.

There were stories about the family in Cornwall. One was about great-grandfather Philip Henry Hammer and his wives. Philip Henry – and he always referred to himself as 'Philip Henry', never just 'Philip' – and his first wife, Jane Opie, had eleven children, but Jane died young and Philip Henry remarried: a middle-aged spinster called Rebecca Jervis. The family story has it that the Hammer children and Rebecca had a strong mutual dislike of each other and that Philip Henry, out of patience with the discord in his house, gave each of the older sons and daughters a gold sovereign and a new outfit of clothes and told them to leave. They scattered to all parts of the world: as far as Tasmania and South Africa, and as near as Wales and Hackney, London. As I grew older and read something of Cornish history, I began to wonder if there was more to the story: was it just a matter of personal relationships, or was it also that from the middle of the nineteenth century the Cornish economy was in decline and many of her people left in search of employment and a better life?

Then there were the old family photographs. My mother kept them safely, and on the back of each, often faded, sepia print had written where and when it was taken, and named every person in each photograph. There were several photos of great-grandfather Philip Henry, of his wife Jane, of some of their children, and of Towan Farm where Philip Henry and Jane spent much of their married life. As I looked at the photos, Philip Henry, his family and Towan began to take on character and life. What more could I find out about them? How did conditions in nineteenth-century Cornwall impact on their lives? This book shows the findings of that research, focusing on the life of a Cornish tenant farmer and his family in the mid to late 1800s, and on those members of the Hammer family with whom, from family stories, I am most familiar.

1

Philip Henry

Philip Henry Hammer was born to John and Elizabeth Hammer on 25 May 1834. He was their eighth child. Elizabeth, known as Betsy, had already given birth to four daughters: Loveday, Maria, Anne, and Elizabeth and three sons: Richard, William, and John. Two more sons, Joseph and Charles Henry, would later be added to the family. Philip Henry's father John was a miner, and the family lived in a cottage in Charlestown Lane, a narrow road on the edge of the busy port of Charlestown, which was then part of the Parish of St Austell in Cornwall.

The origin of the surname Hammer is uncertain. One possible source is derived from the Middle English word 'hamer', meaning a person who lives in a meadow, or a water meadow, or it may have come from a place name, or from the word for a blacksmith, or a maker of hammers.[1] It may also come from an Early German word. These possibilities have no immediately obvious connection to Cornwall, but during the reign of Elizabeth I (1533–1603) several attempts were made to develop the potentially valuable mining sector by encouraging German mining surveyors and engineers to come to England. They were renowned for their mining technology, and in 1564 were given permission to develop mining and smelting in Cornwall and in Devon, York, Lancaster, Cumberland, Westmorland, Gloucester, Worcester, and Wales.[2] Perhaps Philip Henry's family first came to Cornwall as German miners

---

1   *Last name Hammer.* Accessed 17 Oct 2020, https://www.surnamedb.com/Surname/Hammer.

2   *German Miners and Cumbrian Peat Carriers.* Accessed 17 Oct 2020, https://thewildpeak.wordpress.com/2013/04/28/german-miners-and-cumbrian-peat-carriers/.

back in the sixteenth century. The name was first recorded in Cornwall in 1571, soon after the mining experts arrived from Germany, when it was to be found in and around Newquay and Wadebridge. The name was then written as 'Hama', but by the eighteenth century – now spelt as 'Hammer' – it was found more in the St Austell area,[3] where Philip Henry's forebears were born.

Philip Henry's father farmed a small piece of land attached to his cottage, which he first leased in 1832 for an annual rent of £2.14s.0d (2 pounds, 14 shillings). As was then often the custom, the lease was for a period of ninety-nine years or the length of three lives, whichever turned out to be the shorter. When the tenant signed the lease, he named three people, and if ninety-nine years had not passed by the time those three were all dead the lease then expired and the property reverted to the owner. A wise tenant would include the names of the youngest male members of his immediate family so that the lease would have the best chance of being secure for the lifetime of both the tenant and his sons. John Hammer appointed his son Richard, then eleven years old, as the second named person in the lease, and his youngest son John as the third. John junior was only three at the time the lease was signed, and if he survived his early childhood he would add a significant number of years to the lease. The lease comprised:

all that piece of land situate at Charlestown, St. Austell, containing 54 yards, situate on the north side of the road leading to Charlestown Great Road to Holmbush and being parcel of a certain field called Lower Leaf Field in the occupation of William Tremelling, abutting south on the aforesaid road, west on premises lately demised to William Harper, north on the other part of the said field, and east on the hedge separating the said field from the field of Joseph Juch, together with the dwelling house now erected thereon.[4]

---

3   Deacon, Bernard. *The Surnames of Cornwall.* Redruth: CoSERG, 2019, p.75.
4   Cornwall Record Office. *Graham and Graham Solicitors, St. Austell. Lease, Charlestown, St. Austell, 1 January 1832.* This lease was drawn up for the agreement made between representatives of Charlestown Estates and John Hammer.

John Hammer leased his property from Charlestown Estates, a company which owned land and property that had once belonged to Charles Rashleigh, a lawyer, banker, and entrepreneur with mining interests in the St Austell area. It was Charles who had built the harbour at what was then known as West Polmear, but which later became known as 'Charles's town' and, finally, Charlestown. Before Charles Rashleigh built Charlestown Harbour, the population of West Polmear had been just nine fishermen and their families who lived in a few cottages and earned a living by fishing for and salting pilchards, and by assisting with the loading and unloading of the trading vessels that sailed up and down the Cornish coast. As there was no harbour at West Polmear, these vessels had to be beached before any cargo could be moved, and work timed to beat the tide, as when the tide came in work had to stop until the tide turned, leaving the vessels beached once more. This was time-consuming and if the wind blew onshore, or grew in strength, there was always the danger that the beached vessels would be wrecked.

While pilchard fishing and processing was a well-established industry in the St Austell area, the mining of tin, copper and china clay was making an increasingly important contribution to the local economy. To fully exploit the potential of the surrounding mines there was a vital need to replace the practice of beaching by providing a proper harbour. This would offer security from bad weather, consistent deep water where ships could moor up safely, and proper loading and unloading facilities so that ore, china clay and other commodities, including pilchards, could be moved more quickly and efficiently.

Charles Rashleigh was keen to see the development of the local mining industry, and realised that building a harbour at West Polmear would help both his business and the surrounding communities. He employed civil engineer John Smeaton, who had earlier designed the Eddystone Lighthouse, to produce a design for the proposed harbour. Smeaton was an expert in his field and soon completed his proposal. Rashleigh approved the design, and work on the harbour began. In 1791 a pier was constructed, 1792 saw the excavation of the inner dock, and in 1793 a gun battery at the top of Crinnis Cliff on the west side of the harbour was built – this to defend the port from any possible incursion by the French who, during and after the Revolutionary Wars (1792–1802), periodically showed an interest in invading England.

In 1794, a six-mile-long leat – a man-made watercourse – was built from Cam Bridges in the Luxulyan Valley to the port, providing a constant supply of running water via two large reservoir ponds located on the hillside above the harbour. The water from the ponds, as it flowed down to the harbour, was used to power various industrial activities, including the waterwheels for the Charlestown Mill and the china clay crushing plant. This feat of engineering enabled the water level in the harbour to be maintained, prevented the harbour from silting up, and allowed ships to load and unload their cargo efficiently no matter whether the tide was high or low. Several houses were built around the harbour in the same year, and by 1798 the inner basin and dock were complete, while the first lock gates were installed in 1799. As Rashleigh foresaw, the successful completion of Charlestown Harbour enabled the local mining industry to develop, and created employment for many in the St Austell area.

Despite the success of his Charlestown Harbour venture, Charles Rashleigh died almost penniless in 1823. He had largely mismanaged his business affairs, leaving many of his debts unpaid, and owing a large sum of money to local businessman, lawyer and Queen's Counsel, Augustus George Crowder. After protracted legal proceedings Mr Crowder agreed to accept all the leasehold land and buildings in Charlestown in payment of the money owed to him, giving the Crowder family ownership of the port and surrounding village – the property to be re-named Charlestown Estates.

When Philip Henry Hammer was born in 1834, Charlestown's local economy was still benefiting from the increased employment opportunities that came from the construction of the harbour and the resulting development of the local mines. Mine owners were reaping good profits throughout Cornwall, but for a miner life expectancy was short – mining disasters being a regular part of life – and wages were low. In 1847, hungry and angry tin miners and clay workers looted the shops in St Austell to protest about food shortages, an event that Philip

Henry may have witnessed and certainly would have heard about. The food shortages were brought about by a hard winter, the failure of the potato crop due to blight, two years of poor harvest, and an increase in the price of wheat that put basic food staples such as flour and bread beyond the means of the poorly paid miners. By 1851, Philip Henry, then aged seventeen, was working in one of the local mines but, unlike his father and many of his fellow miners, from these modest beginnings he quickly went on to become a miller and then a prosperous farmer of some 140 acres. Where did he acquire the capital that enabled him to improve his standard of living so dramatically?

When Philip Henry was a young man, although the mining industry was largely driving the Cornish economy, miners dissatisfied with their working conditions were beginning to look for better opportunities beyond Cornwall and had started to travel to mining fields elsewhere in the world. Philip Henry was one of them and, with his brothers John and William, in 1854 he left for the booming gold mines of Ballarat in the Central Highlands, Victoria, in Australia. Philip Henry struck it rich, and in early 1858 returned to Cornwall with the profits of his mining adventure to start a new life.[5]

By the time Philip Henry came back to Charlestown, the main business of the port was the production and export of china clay to Liverpool, from where it was transported to the Staffordshire Potteries, to be used in the making of porcelain. Most of the clay pits were grouped around St Austell, so Charlestown, along with the nearby ports of Pentewan, Par and Fowey, became the hub of the Cornish china clay export business. Before the china clay could be shipped out of Charlestown, it had to be transported from the pits down to the harbour, and for this horse-drawn wagons were used. The wagons needed between two and four horses to carry loads of up to 4,500 lbs, and the drivers worked day and night rumbling up and down through the streets of St Austell, through neighbouring Mount Charles and along the Great Charlestown Road to Charlestown Harbour and back to the pits. The Great Charlestown Road was wide enough

---

5   Information taken from a letter written in 1967 by Philip's son Ernest Hammer to his
    daughter Vera, now in the possession of Vera's granddaughter Sandra Burt.

to allow six wagons to travel side by side but was unpaved, so the iron brakes which had to be applied to the wheels of the wagons to slow their downhill journey to the harbour wore deep ruts in the road.

Charlestown Harbour was a busy port, noisy and full of dust from the continuous traffic of the wagons, from the china clay being loaded and shipped out, and from the coal being brought into the harbour to fire the local tin and copper smelting houses, known as blowing houses. A contemporary visitor with a talent for the dramatic phrase writes of the effect this dust had on the landscape of the village:

> What the natural features of Charlestown originally were it is impossible to say, for everything is coated with a white or black dust, and sometimes with both together, the result being a most depressing grey, as of ashes ... At first we could see nothing, but gradually our eyes accustomed themselves to the murk, and we made out that on one side of the harbour vessels were being loaded with china clay, and their crews were as white as millers. On the other side coal was being discharged, and the crews were as black as Erebus. The villagers ... were black or white, according to which side of the port they resided on, while some were both black and white, like magpies.[6]

Philip Henry chose to invest his newfound wealth not in the china clay industry, but in an arable farm with a mill attached. He leased Charlestown Mill, along with a cottage and arable land on Mill Lane, a narrow road that led off from the Great Charlestown Road as it approached Holmbush. Perhaps he remembered the St Austell food riots of 1847, which were partly caused by the high price of wheat: if farmers could make a good living from wheat, then he would grow it and he would mill it.

Philip Henry made his father a partner in his new business, but John Hammer died soon after at the age of sixty-three – a good age for a miner – leaving Philip Henry to live at the mill with his mother Betsy and his brother Charles. Charlestown Mill was a grist mill, its grinding stones

---

6   Noall, Cyril. 'The China Clay Ports', in Noall, *The Story of Cornwall's Ports and Harbours*. Truro: Tor Mark Press, 1970, pp.29–30.

Charlestown Mill and Cottage

powered by a waterwheel that was driven by the leat water as it went on its way down to Charlestown Harbour. The mill ground cattle feed and wheat for Philip Henry's own farm and provided milling services on a commercial basis for other farms in the area. Although mining continued to grow in importance, there were still plenty of farms in the parish needing a miller, as agricultural production had received a boost in 1859 with the completion of a new rail link between Penzance and London which opened up better access to the London market. The rail link was established with the opening of a bridge across the Tamar River, designed by Isambard Kingdom Brunel to enable the extension of the Great Western Railway system into Cornwall. The bridge was named for Queen Victoria's consort, Prince Albert, who opened the bridge on 2 May 1859. The trains stopped at St Austell, and once a regular rail service was established, local farmers could take advantage of Cornwall's relatively warm climate and longer growing season to supply London with both grain and out-of-season fresh produce.

By the early 1860s, Philip Henry was on his way to becoming a successful farmer. His fields totalled thirty acres, stretching from the top of the Great Charlestown Road to the first cottage in neighbouring Holmbush, and he employed four farm labourers to manage the land and run the mill.[7] Now financially stable, he began to think about marrying, and his eye was caught by a slim and attractive girl called Jane Opie, who came from a mining area quite far from Charlestown. In the days when young single women did not usually travel far from home unless to 'go into service' for a wealthy family, or to visit relations living in other parishes, how did they meet?

---

7   Larn, Richard and Bridget Larn. *Charlestown: The History of a Cornish Port.* Charlestown: Larn, 1994, p.93.

2

Jane

Jane Opie was born in 1840 in the Mine Accountant's House in Marke Valley, which lies near to the village of Upton Cross in the parish of Linkinhorne. The daughter of Bennett and Mary Opie, she was the sixth child born to the family and, in the coming years, her mother would go on to give birth to another nine children.

Jane's father was the accountant at the Marke Valley Mine, where he was responsible for keeping the account books, and for paying the miners. He worked in the accounting house, known as the Count House, a small square building located near to his home. The Count House still stands and, although the desks where the Mine Officers worked are gone, the big fireplace that warmed them in the winter is still there, as is the tree that must have given them shade in the summer.

The Marke Valley Mine Count House

The Mine Accountant's House, Marke Valley

Marke Valley runs deep, and copper was first mined here from the streams which run along the valley floor, one of which runs close to the Opie house. But by the 1840s the traditional surface mining had largely been replaced by underground mining, which produced increasing quantities of copper ore. By 1847 the Marke Valley Mine was producing over 1,000 tons of copper ore annually, and by the early 1870s the annual production was 5,000 tons. Business was booming, but it was not until 1877 that the mine was connected to the Liskeard and Caradon Railway.[8] This was opened in 1844 to facilitate the transport of both granite, and copper and tin ores from the mines down to Moorswater, near Liskeard, for onward sea transport out of Looe Harbour. The railway connection came too late for the Marke Valley Mine, which by 1877 was past its peak; ore production fell steadily, and in 1883 it was abandoned.

By the time Jane was eleven years old she had left the Marke Valley and was living with John and Eliza Hawken, who ran a grocer's business in Mount Charles, on the outskirts of St Austell. Jane most likely moved away from home so she could go to school in St Austell, perhaps with the Hawkens' daughter Evelina. St Austell, like most Cornish towns, had a grammar school and may have been one of the few that accepted girl pupils, but grammar schools, although partially supported by charitable endowments from local wealthy families, were mostly fee-paying and attended by children whose parents believed in the value of education and could afford the fees. For poorer members of the community there were the charity schools, and Jane and Evelina may have gone to one of these to gain an elementary education. Many were established by Church of England parish clergy in association with the National Society, while some were set up by the Methodists and other non-conformist denominations in association with the British Society. Only after the passing of the 1870 Education Act were locally elected school boards established and board schools opened, funded from government grants and local rates, to provide elementary education.

---

8   Messenger, Michael John. *Caradon and Looe: the Canal, Railways and Mines; the History of the Liskeard and Looe Union Canal, the Liskeard and Caradon Railway, the Liskeard and Looe Railway, and the Mines and Industries they Served.* Truro: Twelveheads Press, 1978, pp.45, 49.

In 1872, too late for Jane and Evelina, St Austell built the first board school in Cornwall, making education available to a greater number of parish children than ever before.[9]

After completing her schooling, Jane may have stayed in Mount Charles or the St Austell area to be near her father, who by 1861 was living in Lanjeth, also near St Austell, lodging with Henry and Ann Thomas, who both worked in the local china clay pits. Ann may well have been a bal maiden; 'bal' was a Cornish word for a mine, and so the female surface workers were known as bal maidens. Some of these women started work when they were as young as eight or nine, carrying out a wide range of tasks, most of them requiring considerable physical labour.[10] The china clay industry was an important part of St Austell's economy, but there were also several iron mines in the area and, while lodging with the Thomas family, Bennett worked as an iron mine agent at one of the local mines. This, like his work as the accountant at the Marke Valley Mine, was a responsible job; his main task was to manage the mining of as much iron ore as possible at the lowest possible cost for the mine's owners and investors. He had to be continually in touch with all aspects of the mine's working and, as the need arose, he also had to be prepared to enforce unpopular work practices and policies.[11]

If Jane continued to live in Mount Charles after her schooling was complete, it is not too surprising that she met Philip Henry, who was living nearby at Charlestown Mill – perhaps Philip Henry and Bennett were business acquaintances or friends, and Philip Henry met Jane through her father. Whenever and however they met, on 7 August 1862 they were married at St Paul's Parish Church, Charlestown, with Bennett standing as one of the witnesses.[12] Jane was twenty-two, and Philip Henry was twenty-eight.

---

9   Guthrie, Albert. *Cornwall in the Age of Steam*. Padstow: Tabb House, 1994, pp.150–151.
10   Buckley, Allen. *Cornish Bal Maidens*. Redruth: Tor Mark Press, 2010, pp.1, 19.
11   Geevor Tin Mine Museum. *Vocabulary of Cornish Mining Terms*. Penzance: Geevor Tin Mine Museum, 2009.
12   St Austell Parish Genealogy. 'Charlestown Marriages 1860–1862'. Transcribed by J. Mosman, Online Parish Clerk, for the St Austell History & Genealogy website. Accessed 17 October 2020, <http:// freepages.genealogy.rootsweb.ancestry.com/~staustell/ Structure/Genealogy.htm#mar>.

At the time of Philip Henry and Jane's marriage, the church of St Paul's was barely ten years old. By the 1840s, as a result of the expansion of the local mining industry, the population of Charlestown had grown to about 3,000 persons, and the Parish of St Austell, of which Charlestown was a part, had also grown.[13] Recognising the difficulty of managing such a large parish, in 1846 the Diocese of Exeter created two new parishes: the Parish of Treverbyn to the north of St Austell, and the Parish of Charlestown to the south-east. The land on which to build St Paul's for the Parish of Charlestown was given in 1848 by Augustus Crowder, managing director of Charlestown Estates, and the foundation stone was laid in 1849 by Sir Charles Grave Sawle of Penrice House. The church was designed by London architect Christopher Eales and built by Drew and Kitt of St Austell. By 1851 the building was sufficiently complete for consecration and for services to commence, but funds were not enough to complete the church as parishioners might have wished. When services commenced, St Paul's Parish Church was little more than a shell, a condition in which it would remain for some years, so Jane and Philip Henry were married in a church that lacked a steeple and most of its decorative embellishments.[14]

As a miner's son Philip Henry would have been expected to worship at the local Methodist chapel rather than the Anglican parish church. Methodists had been meeting regularly in Charlestown since 1799, and a large Methodist chapel had been in use in the village since 1828. Miners, agricultural labourers, fishermen and other marginalised members of a community were often drawn to Methodism and the teachings of John Wesley, because they stressed the importance of self-help and self-improvement, provided practical support to their members, and helped them cope with the daily hardship of living in rapidly growing mining communities such as St Austell where there were poverty, overcrowding and other social problems. But Philip Henry does not seem at any time to have been drawn to Methodism, and he chose to marry in the new parish church. As a tenant miller and farmer with ambitions to move up

13   St Paul's Church Congregation. *St. Paul's, Charlestown: A Parish Portrait with Historical Notes on Charlestown, Carlyon Bay, Duporth, Mount Charles, Holmbush, Boscundle and Par Moor.* Charlestown: Parish of St Paul's, 2001, pp.10–11.

14   Ibid., p.3.

the social ladder, his religious views probably coincided more with those of the well-established and wealthy gentry and other prosperous farmers and business people, who tended to be church rather than chapel-goers. The Sawles were one such wealthy local family. They had been involved in the building of St Paul's Parish Church, and Philip Henry would later become one of their tenants.

During the first years of their marriage, Philip Henry and Jane lived at Charlestown Mill. Now a man of means, Philip Henry took out a life assurance policy for £200 in February 1864:

With the Briton Medical, General and Life Association for £200 on the life of Philip Henry Hammer, miller, Charlestown Mills, Charlestown, St Austell.[15]

Philip Henry and Jane's first child, Henry, was born at the Mill in 1863, as was their second child, William, usually known as Will, who arrived in 1864. A daughter, Kate, was born in 1865.

With a successful business, an increasing family, and growing ambitions, Philip Henry was now ready to lease a larger property, but it is uncertain in what year the Hammer family moved to Towan Farm. Philip Henry's mother, Betsy, continued to live at the Mill after the death of her husband, but she died in November 1866, so perhaps the move to Towan came after her death. Or perhaps the lease on Charlestown Mill was due to expire and Philip Henry decided that now was the time to move on.

---

15   Cornwall Record Office. *Graham and Graham, Solicitors, St Austell. Life Assurance Policy, Philip Henry Hammer, 27 February 1864.*

3

A Farmer of 140 Acres

Towan Farm, now known as East Towan Farm, is about 3 miles (4.8 km) from Charlestown, where Philip Henry was born. It stands near to the villages of Porthpean and Pentewan, and close to the woodland known as Kings Wood. Connected by narrow lanes to other isolated farms, it is surrounded by irregularly shaped arable fields and pasture. 'Towan' is a Cornish word meaning dune or, more specifically, a mixture of sand and sea rushes – stiff-stemmed reedy grass planted in the sand to stop the sand from drifting.[16] But Towan Farm is not situated within or near to any sand dunes, so it is an unusual choice of name. Originally part of the Royal Manor of Bewingtone,[17] the farm has a long history, and is mentioned in the Domesday Book of 1086 as follows:

> Towan, 3 hides.[18] Land for 20 ploughs; in lordship half of 1 hide; 2 ploughs; 9 slaves, 16 villagers and 40 smallholders with 16 ploughs and 2 and one half hides. Meadow, 2 acres; pasture, 3 leagues long and 1 league wide; woodland, one half league long and 3 furlongs wide. It pays 100 shillings weighed and assayed. 1 cob; 5 unbroken mares; 17 cattle; 200 sheep.[19]

---

16 Maurier, Daphne du. *Vanishing Cornwall*. London: Virago Press, 2007, p.16.
17 Preston-Jones, Ann. *Towan Holy Well, St. Austell, Cornwall: Recording and Repointing.* Truro: Historic Environment Service, Environment and Heritage, Cornwall County Council, November 2006, p.10.
18 A 'hide' is a measurement of land equivalent to about 120 acres.
19 Storey, Tony. 'The Sawle Family of Penrice, Cornwall'. Accessed 19 October 2020, http://www.sole.org.uk/sole2/penrice.htm. (Originally published in the April 2002 edition of *Soul Search*, the journal of the Sole Society.)

Later Towan became part of the Duchy of Cornwall's Manor of Tewington, and the name Towan is possibly a corruption of this name. Tewington was an extensive and valuable property situated on fertile land, which included the Pentewan Valley – the source of a large and profitable stream of tin.[20] In 1596 the manorial centre, which had been presided over by members of the Sawle family since its early days, moved from Towan to neighbouring Penrice, and nothing now remains of the original manor house.

Perhaps through connections built up with the Sawle family by his regular attendance at St Paul's Parish Church, Philip Henry learnt that Towan was available, and entered into a lease agreement with the Sawle family. In the later nineteenth century, farms were usually leased out for fixed terms of either seven, fourteen or twenty-one years. This contrasted with earlier years when a lease was usually – as we saw in the case of Philip Henry's father John – for ninety-nine years or for three named lives. Fourteen years was the lease period most frequently used, and this was probably the term agreed between Philip Henry and the Sawle family.[21]

As the tenant, Philip Henry was responsible for the good management of all that he leased, both land and buildings, and many leases incorporated a 'good agricultural practices' clause that would have to be met if the lease were to be renewed. As there was no automatic renewal of a farm lease, a short lease gave little security to the tenant and his family beyond the length of their current fixed term.

As shown by the *St Austell Tithe Map and Apportionment* of 1841, which names each of Towan's fields, the farm was largely given over to the cultivation of arable land.[22]

---

20 Preston-Jones, Ann. *Towan Holy Well, St. Austell, Cornwall: Recording and Repointing.* Truro: Historic Environment Service, Environment and Heritage, Cornwall County Council, November 2006, p.10.

21 The lease document between the Sawle family and Philip Henry Hammer has not been traced, but a similar lease for Towan taken out by William Thomas in 1853 was for fourteen years.

22 Carveth, Richard. *St. Austell Tithe Map and Apportionment 1841.* The tithe maps and accompanying survey books (apportionments) were drawn up under the Tithe Commutation Act of 1836 which commuted tithe payments in kind to cash payments. Richard Carveth was the surveyor who completed the survey.

Towan's fields in 1841

Name and description of lands	State of cultivation
Salters	Arable
Mathews Park	Arable
Dwelling House, Outhouses, Mowhay, and Waste	
Mowhay Meadow	Arable
Slade Meadow	Arable
Great Meadow	Arable
Cooks Field	Arable
Hill	Arable and waste
Chapel Park	Arable
Chapel Close	Arable
Dryers Meadow	Arable
Moor	Pasture
Orchard	Orchard
Little Horse Park	Arable
Great Horse Park	Arable
Long Close	Arable
Three Acres	Arable
Twelve Acres	Arable
Hay Field	Arable

The home where Philip Henry lived with his family was a pleasantly proportioned and substantial granite farmhouse built in the latter part of the eighteenth century, when a building style based on classical Greek architecture, which had already been adopted by the Cornish gentry for their grand residences, was beginning to influence the building of smaller houses. As V. M. and F. J. Chesher note in their book *The Cornishman's House*:

> *the circulation of [architectural] pattern books made the new ideas available to country builders. As a result, by the middle of the eighteenth century, a style of medium-sized house had emerged which represented the scaled-down version of the new architectural concepts … The greatest innovation in the layout was the 'double plan', with the house built two rooms deep, instead of the old arrangement of rooms in a row. This made possible an entirely new type of interior, which reflected a changing social outlook and pattern of household life. The ideal home of the country middle classes had finally disposed of the hall-house idea, with its central communal living room as the focus. In the new dwelling the hall had shrivelled to nothing more than an entrance lobby, housing the stairs – which had found a place in the centre of the design at last – giving separate access to the various rooms. The 'reception' rooms, parlour and new-style dining room, monopolised the front of the building: at the back were the kitchen quarters, banished from view, and the servants with them.[23]*

Towan farmhouse has many of the features of the Greek classical revival style. It is two rooms deep, with a slate roof, a central doorway, four narrow chimneys – one rising from each corner – and regularly spaced windows with sash frames. Remnants of the earlier Gothic style of architecture can be seen in the arched head of the front door which was repeated in miniature at the top of the wooden window frames. The windows and part of the front door can be seen in the photograph on page 56 of Philip

---

23   Chesher, V.M. and F. J. Chesher. *The Cornishman's House: An Introduction to the History of Traditional Domestic Architecture in Cornwall*. Truro: D. Bradford Barton Ltd, 1968, pp.93–94.

Henry standing outside Towan farmhouse with his son and daughter-in-law.

Flanking the entrance hall is a parlour and dining room, both used on special occasions. These two rooms are separated by a hallway from where a main staircase leads upstairs to six bedrooms. At the back of the house is another narrow staircase, which at the time gave separate access to one bedroom for the use of the live-in labourers and servants. While Jane lived at Towan there were two live-in male farm labourers and two live-in female domestic servants, so it is likely that the two female servants were allowed to use the main staircase and slept in one of the bedrooms in the main house.

At the back of the house is a large farmhouse kitchen and living area where all the family, as well as live-in farm labourers and domestic servants, would eat together. Next to the kitchen is a pantry with a stone floor and shelves which was used to keep food cool. The kitchen had an open fire, later a kitchen range, fuelled by turf, furze,[24] wood, or imported Welsh coal. In the chimney recess at one side of the fire would have been a cloam baking oven with a sealable earthenware – and later iron – door. To use the oven, the inside was first filled with hot ashes from the fire, then wood faggots, furze, or blackthorn were added, set alight and blown with a bellows to increase the heat until the inside of the oven had turned white. The ashes were then quickly raked out and bread or a joint of meat put in to bake. After these, smaller items such as pasties were baked before the oven cooled.

An entrance from the kitchen would have given easy access to the stable area, so that the live-in farm labourers, who spent their evenings in the farm kitchen, could easily attend to the horses. There would also have been an outside water pump and a laundry area. To the side of the house are several well-constructed granite farm buildings which would have been used for housing chickens, the house cow, and a few pigs. There was also a thatched one-storey barn and a pond for watering the horses and any other livestock.

---

24   A thorny evergreen shrub, with yellow flowers, also known as gorse.

Towan Farm

After moving to Towan, Philip Henry and Jane continued to add to their family. In 1867 Jane gave birth to Philip, in 1869 to Anne – known as Annie – and in 1870 to Charles Henry. The son she bore in 1872 was called Bennett, after her father, and given Arthur as his second name. But he died when he was little more than a baby, by which time Jane was already pregnant with another son, born in 1873 – a son who would also be called Arthur. Ernest arrived in 1874 and Frederick George in 1875.

During the 1870s there were many mouths to feed at Towan. There were Philip Henry, Jane and their children. There were the two labourers: Richard Reep and John Garland, aged twenty-two and fifteen respectively. There were the two domestic servants: Harriet Werry, aged twenty-one, and her sister Sarah, aged thirteen. There were also all those who came to work at harvest time, during the hay season, or at any other busy time on the farm when extra hands were needed to finish the work.

Jane was responsible for cooking everything except for the barley bread, which was usually made by the servants, Harriet and Sarah, whose first job was to make the leaven, or rising agent for the bread – a long process. An old Cornish recipe from the days when open fires were used gives the following instructions:

> *To make the Leaven mix a small quantity of barley flour with warm water into a dough. Form it into a round shape, like a pat of butter; make a dent in the centre with the thumb, about half-way through. Set the dough on a plate, cross it lightly twice, like a hot-cross bun, and fill the dent with warm water. Set it aside for a few days when the dough will have fermented and split like an over-ripe fruit. It is then ready to use instead of yeast.*[25]

The barley bread is then made with the leaven:

> *in the usual way with warm water and a little salt. When the bread has been sufficiently kneaded, take a small piece of the dough and*

---

25   Martin, Edith. *Cornish Recipes Ancient and Modern*. Truro: Cornwall Federation of Women's Institutes, 1929, p.12.

prepare it for leaven against the next baking day. Cover the newly-mixed bread with a cloth and set in a warm place. When risen, form into circular-shaped loaves and bake under a kettle[26] on the hearth.[27]

Food was simple but varied. On Sundays, a typical meal might be a piece of beef put on to boil with vegetables, a rabbit or two, a potato pie with plenty of beef in it, or a rib of pork. As Towan was largely arable, beef would have been bought from the local butcher, although there would have been some sheep and a few pigs to provide lamb, mutton and pork, and enough dairy cows to provide milk. On Saturdays, and sometimes during the week, there were pilchards and potatoes with bread and butter. Fresh fish was eaten several times a week in the summer when hake, whiting, mackerel and pilchards were supplied by the fishwives – the women who waited with their baskets at the harbour for the fish caught during the night and then brought them out to nearby farms early in the morning. Mackerel and pilchards were a Cornish staple, and here are two recipes that Jane might have used:

Marinated Mackerel

4 or more mackerel	Sprig of thyme
2 chopped bay leaves	1 onion
6 cloves	10 peppercorns
Blade of mace	Salt and vinegar

Clean and prepare mackerel and arrange in a pie dish, chop the onion and parsley and sprinkle over the fish. Add other ingredients with salt to taste. Pour over sufficient vinegar to cover well and bake in moderate

---

26 This is a bake kettle, also known as a Dutch oven, not a kettle used to boil water. It is a large, sturdy cooking pot with a tight-fitting lid, usually made of cast iron which can be used for baking. When the bread is placed in the kettle and the lid placed on top, the kettle is put in the hot coals of the open fire, with hot coals also placed on top of the lid. The coals on the lid are replaced each time they cool, until the bread is cooked.

27 Martin, Edith. *Cornish Recipes Ancient and Modern.* Truro: Cornwall Federation of Women's Institutes, 1929, p.12.

oven for 40 or 50 minutes. When cooked put fish carefully on a dish and strain vinegar over them. Leave until cold and serve.[28]

Scrowled[29] Pilchards

Clean fish and split quite open, mix teaspoonful salt, sugar and pepper, sprinkle well over them, and leave over-night. Then scrowl on gridiron over a clear fire.[30]

Salted fish was used when no fresh fish was available, first soaked in fresh water to get rid of the salt, then cooked, again often with potatoes. There might also be broth made with fat pork and dumplings and sprinkled with marigold flowers. Another popular dish was a pie made with potatoes and slices of fat pork, covered with a thick pastry crust.

There were of course pasties, which came with various fillings both sweet and savoury. There was the traditional mixture of beef, potatoes, swede, and onions or, to name but a few of the other popular fillings: pork, herbs with bacon and eggs, mackerel, rabbit, apple, or jam. To make the pasties, Jane may have used a recipe similar to this:

[For the pastry] 1 lb. flour, 1 lb. lard and suet, 1 teaspoonful salt, mix with water … When pastry is made, roll out about 1/4-inch-thick, and cut into rounds with a plate to the size desired. Lay the rounds on the pastry board with half of the round over the rolling pin and put in the fillings, damp the edges lightly and fold over into a semi-circle. Shape the pasty nicely and crimp the extreme edges where it is joined between the finger and thumb. Cut a slit in the centre of the pasty … and bake in a quick oven, so that it keeps its shape.[31]

---

28 Ibid., p.29.
29 To scrowl means to grill over an open fire.
30 Martin, Edith. *Cornish Recipes Ancient and Modern.* Truro: Cornwall Federation of Women's Institutes, 1929, p.30.
31 Ibid., pp.31–32.

When a pig was killed there was pig's fry made from the various kinds of offal, and muggety pie made with the pig's intestines. The old recipe is quite simple:

> Take the pots[32] of a pig, wash them and place in a pie-dish with plenty of onions, pepper and salt. Cover with pastry and bake.[33]

For vegetables, in addition to potatoes, there were turnips, carrots, cabbages, onions and leeks, which were often made into a leeky, or likky, pie like this:

12 leeks	2 eggs
1 lb. green bacon	Some milk for gravy
1 lb. cream	

> Take the leeks and cut in small pieces, scald about ten minutes in boiling water. Cut bacon in very thin slices. Put a layer of bacon in the bottom of pie-dish, then a layer of leeks, and continue each layer until dish is full, season with pepper and salt. Cover with suet crust. Have ready the cream, two well-beaten eggs, beaten separately (whites and yolks). When pie is [nearly] cooked, take off crust and drain off [nearly] all liquid from the pie and substitute the cream and [beaten] eggs.[34]

Dessert was sometimes a junket, which is made from milk, a little sugar and rennet, an extract made from the fourth stomach of calves, kids or lambs, which causes the milk to set. When the junket was ready, some grated nutmeg was sprinkled on the top. Pies were always popular, made with apples, blackberries, gooseberries, or whatever fruit was in season – the fruit mixed with sugar and the whole pie topped with clotted or clouted cream.

The preparation of clotted cream was a regular part of kitchen life and, as this recipe shows, its preparation took some time:

---

32 Pots are the intestines of a pig.
33 Martin, Edith. *Cornish Recipes Ancient and Modern*. Truro: Cornwall Federation of Women's Institutes, 1929, p.39.
34 Ibid., p.57.

Use new milk and strain at once, as soon as milked, into shallow pans. Let it stand for 24 hours in winter and 12 hours in summer. Then put the pan on the [range or] stove, or, better still, into a steamer containing water, and let it slowly heat until the cream begins to show a raised ring round the edge. When sufficiently cooked place in a cool dairy and leave for 12 or 24 hours. Great care must be taken in moving the pans, so that the cream is not broken, both in putting on the fire and taking off.[35]

The clotted cream was taken off the top of the pan with a skimmer, a long-handled ladle full of holes that allowed the skim milk to run back into the pan. Some of the cream was then made into butter in a round wooden butter churn that was turned by hand until the cream, with the addition of a little salt, became a deep yellow butter.

Various kinds of cake were served with tea. There was the traditional saffron cake, made with yeast and containing saffron and plenty of currants. Saffron was an expensive but popular spice in Cornwall, and it is said that it was first brought to Cornwall by Phoenicians from the Eastern Mediterranean as early as 400 BCE, when their traders came to buy Cornish tin. Another possibility is that saffron may have arrived much later – in the fourteenth century, when there was demand for tin from Spain, where the spice was a regular ingredient in local cuisine. This is one of the many recipes for saffron cake:

Take 2 lbs. flour, 1 lb. fat (lard, butter, or a mixture of these), 1 lb. sugar, 2 oz. mixed peel finely shredded, 1 lb. currants or sultanas (or mixed), 1 oz. yeast, warm milk, or milk and water, ½ drachm[36] of saffron threads.[37]

To prepare saffron, take half drachm and cut very fine with scissors, pour over half cup boiling water and steep overnight.

Rub fat thoroughly into flour, add sugar and good pinch of salt. Put yeast in a cup with teaspoonful sugar, add little warm milk—not hot, but more than tepid. When yeast rises in cup make a pit in flour

---

35   Ibid., p.6.
36   A drachm, or dram, measures 1/16 of an ounce.
37   The dried aromatic stigmas of the crocus plant – crocus sativus.

and pour the yeast in with little more warm milk, turn a little flour over it. When this cracks and the yeast sponges through, mix into a soft dough with the hand, using milk as required. Add saffron when mixing. Add fruit, put a warm plate on it and stand it in a warm place until the mixture raises the plate and appears light and spongy.

Part may be made into buns or the whole baked in cake tins. In either case allow to 'rise' for a short time before baking. Buns 15 to 20 minutes, cakes three-quarters or one hour, according to size.[38]

There was seedy cake – a sponge cake containing caraway seeds – and gingerbread was popular, as was heavy – or hevva – cake made from flour mixed with butter or sour cream, currants, and a pinch of salt:

1 lb. flour	*6 ozs. currants*
1 lb. fresh butter	*Pinch of salt*

Take 1/3lb. butter and rub into the flour, make it into a stiff dough with cold water; having added the currants and salt, roll it out on the board; take another 1/3lb. butter and lay it in small pieces over the dough, flour and fold it up, roll again twice, adding the remainder of the butter, then roll it out finally an inch thick ; score the surface in small diamonds, brush over with milk and bake for half an hour in a quick oven.[39]

All this food was usually washed down with tea or cider. Towan had an orchard and cider would have been made for the family, the labourers, the servants, and those who came to help with the harvest. Jane probably made wine with elderberries, blackberries, gooseberries, and blackcurrants, and Philip Henry would have brewed his own beer. Spirits such as gin were kept in the house, as it was the custom to offer food and a variety of drink, to visitors, and gin was used to make drinks such as sloe gin, which requires steeping pricked sloes in the gin with a little sugar for several months,[40] and

---

38 Martin, Edith. *Cornish Recipes Ancient and Modern.* Truro: Cornwall Federation of Women's Institutes, 1929, p.24.
39 Ibid., pp.15–16.
40 Ibid., p.57.

mahogany, or blackstrap, made with a mixture of two parts gin to one part treacle beaten well together. For those who preferred the flavour of brandy to gin, Jane would have made mead, also known as metheglin or sweet drink:

> [Take] 4 lbs. honey, 1 gallon water, boil it one hour; skim well, then add 1 oz. hops to every gallon ; boil it half an hour longer, and let it stand till next day. Put it into a cask or bottles. To every gallon add 1 gill brandy. Stop it lightly till fermentation is over, then stop it close ; keep one year before use.[41]

Those who liked the added flavour of aromatic plants such as thyme, rosemary, sweet-briar, and heather, boiled them in the water before adding the honey.

Kate and Annie, the daughters in the family, assisted with the housework, helped to milk the family cow, and looked after the chickens. During the hay season and at harvest time the girls worked in the fields alongside the older sons, Henry, Will, Philip and Charles, and the labourers Richard and John. An agricultural labourer's work was varied, and they worked long hours. Richard and John would have been responsible for mucking out and watering the animals kept on the farm for family use; keeping the farm implements and harness for the horses in working order; helping plough, harrow, plant, weed and harvest the crops, and repairing the farm buildings. The domestic servants, Harriet and Sarah, did the bulk of the housework: doing the laundry, mending the family's clothes, bringing in the furze and turf for the fires, and feeding the family pigs and chickens. They also helped milk the family cows and, like everyone else, helped in the fields during harvesting.

As Towan was an arable farm, hay, barley and wheat were planted regularly, the hay to be sold for the feeding of livestock in the winter months, the barley and wheat ground into flour. Potatoes were a major crop, a mainstay of the local diet, and well suited to the growing conditions of the relatively warm and damp Cornish climate. Turnips were grown in rotation to add nitrogen content to the soil and to feed animals, and

---

41 Ibid., p.53.

methods for improving the soil included the use of well-rotted animal manure, sea sand, seaweed, and spoilt pilchards.

Farm implements were pulled by one or more horses or mules – animals without which no farm could function – and included a plough, a harrow for breaking down the soil after ploughing, a muck spreader, stone rollers for levelling out the ground, hoes for weeding between the rows of root crops, a wain for carrying hay, a dray or sled, various carts for transporting hay and corn and other crops, and a threshing machine to separate the corn from the chaff. There was also a wooden frame, known as a crook, which was slung over the back of a mule or horse, and used for carrying small quantities of wood or corn sheaves.

Harvest time was busy at Towan, as it was on all farms. Everyone on the farm helped, but temporary labourers who were skilled scythe-men were in great demand and would be sought out well in advance of the start of the harvest. The scythe-men took great pride in having a blade that would cut the most before it had to be whetted or sharpened, and spent a good deal of time choosing the right whetting stone with which to sharpen their scythe. The team of scythe-men worked together under the guidance of the most skilled and experienced labourer, their scythes making strokes in unison as they moved across the field. They were followed by women and boys who gathered up the corn, and then by the men who bound the corn into sheaves.

The reaping of the last few stands of corn in the field was marked by an event known as 'crying the neck' – a custom that came from the days when thanks were given to the spirit of the corn for a harvest safely brought in, and which let the surrounding farms know that the harvest had been successfully completed.[42] At Towan, as the scythe-man leading the team cut the last stalks, known as the neck, and raised them above his head, he would shout, 'I hav'et! I hav'et! I hav'et!' The rest of the harvesters would then reply, 'What hav'ee? What hav'ee? What hav'ee?' The scythe-man would answer, 'A neck! A neck! A neck!' Then all the harvesters would shout, 'Hip hip hurrah! Hurrah for the neck! Hurrah for Mr Hammer!' The neck of corn was then plaited, decorated with flowers, and carried to

---

42 Courtney, M.A. *Cornish Feasts and Folklore*. Wakefield: EP Publishing, 1973, p.76.

Jane's kitchen where it would be tied up over the chimney-piece until the next harvest. The Neck Supper was held the same evening, and all the men, women and children who had helped bring in the harvest gathered in the farmhouse kitchen. There they ate well – perhaps starting with a beef broth with vegetables, followed by a large joint of beef and potatoes, then apple pies spread with sugar and clotted cream, all washed down with cider or beer for the men and tea for the women and children.

After reaping, the corn sheaves were set up into shocks or stooks of about eight sheaves to ripen and dry. The shocks were then carted to the mowhay – the enclosed yard close to the farmyard where the ricks or stacks of corn were built. The rick was built on a framework of boards raised a few feet off the ground by steads – large mushroom-shaped stones whose shape helped prevent rats from reaching the stack – and, to protect the corn from rain, the rick was thatched over with corn straw or rushes. The completion of the ricks was reason for another supper, the Harvest Supper, when all those who had helped at Towan celebrated the successful completion of the harvest. Here, following a meal that included beef, mutton, chicken and potatoes, a special pudding – similar to a figgy or Christmas pudding – was eaten. During the following winter, the sheaves were brought from the mowhay to the barn, where a horse-driven threshing machine separated out the grain.

The Neck Supper and the Harvest Supper were only two of many celebrations that took place throughout the year. One of the most important was the Parish Feast, and for most mining communities this was more important than either Easter or Christmas. After the traditional church service, friends and neighbours were invited to eat a special meal, and the festivities would continue as the young men of the parish took part in hurling[43] and wrestling competitions.[44] One of the most popular of the many Parish Feasts was the St Austell Feast,[45] which was held on

---

43 Hurling is one of Cornwall's oldest games, dating back many hundreds of years. It is played between two teams, each trying – by whatever means necessary – to keep possession of a cricket-sized ball made of silver-coated apple wood.

44 Rule, John. *Cornish Cases: Eessays in 18th and 19th Century History*. Southampton: Clio Publishing, 2006, pp.269–270.

45 The name St Austell is derived from St Austol, an early Welsh Christian who lived for most of his life in Brittany.

the Thursday after Whitsunday,[46] and the Hammers may well have made the journey from Towan to St Austell to take part in the festival.

There were numerous celebrations throughout the whole of the Twelve Days of Christmas. On Christmas Eve, a large log of wood, selected some months earlier and kept dry, was brought into the farmhouse and put on the fire, kindled with a piece of charred wood saved from last year's log. This was known as the Christmas Stock or Christmas Block, and was kept burning for the whole of the Christmas season. A Christmas Bush was made of two wooden hoops fastened together at right angles, and decorated with furze and evergreens which at night was lit by a candle fixed inside the hoops.[47] In some households it was the custom to make a batch of specially-shaped saffron cakes on Christmas Eve. These had two layers, with a small cake fixed on top of the large one, and it was bad luck to cut and eat them until Christmas Day.[48]

There was always plenty of food and drink for the Christmas dinner, when baked ham and roast goose, figgy pudding, cake, and a type of mince pie, called a sweet giblet pie, was served. This pie was a traditional part of the meal. To make it:

Take one or two sets of goose giblets, apples, spice, currants, raisins, moist sugar and nutmeg. Prepare and clean all ingredients, put together in a large pie-dish, cover with pastry and bake well in a good oven.[49]

There was dancing and singing of carols throughout the Christmas season, and a choir from a neighbouring church or chapel might visit Towan, where they would sing carols in return for food and drink, or for money. The Cornish have a long tradition of carol, or curl, singing and some of the words and tunes that are used are very old.[50]

---

46 *St Austell Feast Week*. Accessed 17 October 2020, https://www.cornwallforever.co.uk/year/st-austell-feast-week.

47 Courtney, M.A. *Cornish Feasts and Folklore*. Wakefield: EP Publishing, 1973, p.12.

48 Ibid., pp.11–12.

49 Ibid., p.49.

50 Ibid., p.12.

Towan had an apple orchard, so perhaps the following tradition, which M.A. Courtney describes in *Cornish Feasts and Folklore*, was a regular feature of the Hammer Christmas season:

In some places the parishioners walk in procession, visiting the principal orchards in the parish. In each orchard one tree is selected, as the representative of the rest; this is saluted with a certain form of words, which have in them a form of an incantation. They then sprinkle the tree with cider, or dash a bowl of cider against it, to ensure its bearing plentifully the ensuing year.

In other places the farmers and their servants only assemble on the occasion, and after immersing the apples in cider hang them on the apple-trees. They then sprinkle the trees with cider; and after uttering a formal incantation, they dance round it (or rather round them) and return to the farmhouse to conclude these solemn rites with copious draughts of cider.[51]

If the family went into St Austell or Charlestown at this time of year, they may well have met up with the groups of mummers known as 'Guise Dancers' who roamed the streets. The mummers were all disguised – hence the name – in outlandish clothes and strange masks and, as they were not easy to recognise, '*often behaved in such an unruly manner that women and children were afraid to venture out*.'[52]

The Christmas season came to an end with Twelfth Day and Twelfth Night, or Epiphany, once the day when Christmas Day celebrations were held. The sharing of the Twelfth Day cake was an important part of the holiday, and before the cake went into the oven a wedding ring, a sixpenny piece, and a thimble were added to the mixture. When baked, the cake was shared between the guests and family to see what the future would bring. Whoever found the wedding ring would be married in the coming year. Whoever found the thimble would never be married. And whoever found the sixpence would die rich.

---

51   Courtney, M.A. *Cornish Feasts and Folklore*. Wakefield: EP Publishing, 1973, pp.14–15.
52   Ibid., p.16.

Later in the year, another tradition was to visit one of the nearby holy wells to drop a coin or a bent pin into the spring water, making a wish as you did so. Cornwall has many holy wells, all supplied by shallow springs[53] which provide a continual supply of pure water and from pre-Christian times have been credited with special powers. As the Rev. Lane-Davies notes:

> *Pure water, so essential to life must always have been regarded with wonder and veneration. A spring was 'alive'. Some mysterious power caused it to bubble forth … Was the living water itself a powerful living entity or did it derive its character and power from an indwelling spirit? In any case the spring must be reverenced.*[54]

As Christianity came to Cornwall during the fifth and sixth centuries, teachers and holy men arrived, many from Ireland and Wales, and some settled near a spring which was already a recognised place of worship and provided a reliable source of fresh water for day-to-day use. Gradually the power of the spring became associated with Christian beliefs and usage and, in many cases, with the name of the resident holy man – often known as a saint, even though not recognised as such by the Church of Rome.

At Towan Farm, the nearest holy well – known as Chapel Well, Towan Holy Well, or Towan Well – was just across the fields from the farmhouse. It is thought to date from the fifteenth century and that, as suggested by the name Chapel Well and the names of two of Towan's fields, Chapel Park and Chapel Close,[55] it had a chapel nearby at one time. By the nineteenth century the well's popularity as a place of veneration had faded, and it lay buried in the surrounding undergrowth, largely

---

53 Leggat, P.O. and D.V. Leggat. *The Healing Wells: Cornish Cults and Customs*. Redruth: Dyllansow Truran, 1987, p.8.
54 Lane-Davies, Rev. A. *Holy Wells of Cornwall: a Guide*. np: Federation of Old Cornwall Societies, 1970, p.2.
55 Carveth, Richard. *St. Austell Tithe Map and Apportionment 1841*.

forgotten. In 1882 it was visited by Doctor Thomas Quiller-Couch[56] as part of his ongoing project to record Cornwall's holy wells. He writes:

This well is on Towan Farm, a little south of St. Austell town … Winding to the left, close by a wayside inn with a curious signboard, 'The London Apprentice', – a name suggestive of some wild roistering and lawless riot, or of venture and success – then, turning up a hill, long and steep … I arrived at the farmhouse, where I luckily found an intelligent boy, who knew all about the well, and where it was.[57]

Given the date of Doctor Quiller-Couch's visit, the 'intelligent boy' must have been one of the younger Hammer boys.

Having found the well, the Doctor goes on to describe it:

The well was buried in a bush growth of ivy and bramble … By carefully turning back as much of this lavish drapery as I could, I made out a stately well, built of shaped and shapely granite slabs. The doorway was finished upwards by a chamfered, I should say equilateral arch. The water flooded the whole of the enclosed space, the roof was arched like the doorway, and in the end wall was a neat and large bracket pedestal, evidently for the image of a saint … The [Hammer] boy had never heard of elf or saint in connection with it, and could tell me no story of its ever being frequented for health or fortune-telling. Its position and surroundings spoke of long neglect and desolation. The massive nature of its construction has wonderfully preserved this once beautiful fountain from destruction, and very little cost and care would restore it. I made its condition known to its owner, Sir C. Graves-Sawle, Bart., of Penrice.[58][59]

---

56 Thomas Quiller-Couch (died 1884) was a Cornish medical doctor, folklorist, and historian. He was the father of the well-known author, poet and literary critic Sir Arthur Quiller-Couch (1863–1944) who wrote under the pseudonym Q.

57 Quiller-Couch, Mabel and Lillian Quiller-Couch. *Ancient and Holy Wells of Cornwall.* London: Charles J. Clark, 1894, p.30.

58 Ibid., p.31.

59 Chapel Well, Towan, was restored by the St Austell Old Cornwall Society in 1937, but later again became overgrown. In 2004, the roof of the well was repointed by members of the Pentewan Old Cornwall Society.

Towan Holy Well

Easter celebrations began early in Cornwall. On Good Friday, which in England was traditionally a day of mourning, Cornish families celebrated Goody Friday with a special feast which included Easter saffron buns. Families went for walks to enjoy the spring weather, to gather cockles – or trigg-meat – and to picnic.

While he enjoyed the festivals and celebrations, Philip Henry never forgot the importance of developing Towan as a profitable enterprise. A photograph taken of Philip Henry, Jane and either Richard Reep or John Garland shows a well-kept farmyard. Although the barn was thatched, the roof of the building behind them is made with galvanised iron sheets, a material that had just started to come into use – like many successful Victorian businessmen, Philip Henry was quick to utilise new developments in manufacturing techniques. The cart in the photograph is of the same design as those used to transport tin, copper, and china clay down the Great Charlestown Road to Charlestown Harbour: sturdily designed and capable of carrying heavy loads when pulled by enough mules or horses. Philip Henry looks proudly at the camera, confident that the photograph will record his achievements: he has risen from miner to successful farmer, and from the photograph we know that he has a capable wife and a farm with substantial buildings, and employs farm labourers. Not for him a formal portrait of the Hammer family standing stiffly in their Sunday best. Richard – or John – appears relaxed if a little shy. Jane watches the photographer with a confident if slightly impatient expression, hands clasped behind her back as she inspects the photographer and his new-fangled, cumbersome equipment. She has left her domestic duties to put on a clean apron for the occasion, but is ready to get back to her kitchen.

The photograph was taken some time between 1866 – about the time when the Hammers moved to Towan Farm – and 1877. Given the recent development of photography, it is quite an early image. The photographer may well have been another member of the Hammer family, because in the 1873 *Kelly's Directory for Cornwall* under the listing of tradespeople in St Austell is listed: 'Hammer, William Henry, photographer, Bullring'.[60] Perhaps William Hammer took this photo.

Left to right: Philip Henry, Richard Reep
or John Garland, and Jane, at Towan

As a successful businessman and large leaseholder, Philip Henry had the right to vote and, along with other prominent members of the community, played his part in the running of local affairs. One of his duties was as an elected member of the Board of Guardians which managed

---

60 *Kelly's Directory for Cornwall 1873: St Austell*. London: Kelly and Co., 1872, p.818.

the St Austell Poor Law Union.[61] These unions were established after an 1834 Act of Parliament transferred the responsibility of looking after the poor from the local parish church to the government, which then made each civil parish a member of a union of parishes, each Poor Law Union having a membership of about twenty parishes.

Philip Henry and Jane were raising a family of nine children, with Jane apparently suffering no ill effects from her frequent childbearing. By late 1876, Jane was again pregnant, giving birth to a daughter in the middle of 1877. She was named Emily Opie and she was to be Philip Henry and Jane's last child, because having given birth to Emily, Jane died at the end of June. She was only thirty-five years old. Emily clung on to life only until the middle of July. Jane and her children Bennett and Emily were buried together in the churchyard of St Paul's Parish Church, Charlestown, where Philip Henry and Jane had been married just fifteen years before. The wording on the headstone Philip Henry erected for Jane and their two children reads:

In Memory of Jane
beloved wife of P.H. Hammer of Towan,
St. Austell died June 30th 1877 aged thirty five years
also
Bennett Arthur
son of the above died January 3rd 1873
also
Emily
daughter of the above died July 16th 1877
In hope of a joyful resurrection[62]

Philip Henry was left to care for the family. When Jane died, the eldest child, Henry, was fourteen, while the youngest, Frederick – usually known as Fred – was only two years old. The two girls, Kate and Annie, were

---

61   'St. Austell. The Guardians', *Royal Cornwall Gazette*, Saturday 27 March 1875, p.6.
62   Cornwall Family History Society, 'Monumental Inscriptions Database'. Accessed 17 October 2020, http://www.cornwallfhs.com/. Also, the Hammer family headstone in St Paul's Parish Church churchyard.

twelve and eight respectively. Kate, as the elder of the two girls, would have taken on much of the responsibility for helping to raise the younger children and for feeding the family, the labourers, and the domestic servants. By 1881, the census returns show that the eldest son, Henry, was now a pupil teacher, while Will and Kate helped run the farm with the help of only one servant, nineteen-year-old Mary Ann Vane.[63] Funds now seem to have been in short supply at Towan because in September 1880 Philip Henry borrowed fifty pounds from the successful merchant Samuel Moss of Boscundle, St Austell:

on the security of a promissory note and deeds of two dwelling houses and plot of land, and life assurance policy of 200 pounds.[64]

Perhaps it had been Jane who kept the account books for Philip Henry. As the daughter of a mine officer responsible for running the Count House at the Marke Valley Mine, she most likely grew up with some practical knowledge of accounting which she would have put to good use at Towan. But with her death there may have been no one to take on her accounting responsibilities. The financial management of the farm probably suffered and, in order to continue farming Towan, or renew his lease, Philip Henry found it necessary to take out a loan.

About five years after Jane's death, with his lease renewed and Towan Farm a secure tenancy for a further term, Philip Henry – struggling to bring up his young family and manage his farm without a wife – began to give some thought to marrying again. In St Austell he met Rebecca Jervis, an unmarried woman of about fifty years of age, and on 14 June 1883 he married her in Holy Trinity Parish Church, St Austell. The two witnesses to the marriage were Rebecca's brother, John T. Jervis, and Philip Henry's sister, Elizabeth Hammer.[65]

---

63   The National Archives of the UK. Public Record Office. *England Census 1881: Class: RG11; Piece: 2302; Folio: 41; Page: 22.*

64   Cornwall Records Office. *Graham and Graham, Solicitors, St. Austell. Documents Relating to the Estate of Samuel Moss of Boscundle, St Austell.*

65   Julia Mosman, email message to the author, 15 October 2008. Julia Mosman is the online parish clerk for St Austell.

4

A Gold Sovereign and a New Suit

Rebecca Jervis was born in Coggeshall, Essex, in 1833, the eldest child of Henry and Susannah Jervis. Her father was a coachbuilder and her mother a milliner. By the time Rebecca was eighteen, the family had moved to Lady Lane, St Matthew, near Ipswich in Suffolk, where Rebecca learnt millinery from her mother and helped her to make hats. She later moved away from home to work as a milliner in a hat shop in Ipswich, a thriving business in the Old Buttermarket that employed ten milliners.

By the time she met Philip Henry, Rebecca had, for some reason, moved from Suffolk to Cornwall, and was perhaps working as a milliner for Mrs Caroline Loye, a dressmaker and milliner who had a business on Fore Street in St Austell.[66] Rebecca and Philip Henry seem an unlikely match. Did they genuinely care for each other? Were they looking for companionship in their later years? Was Philip Henry looking for a housekeeper to help him raise his family and manage Towan? Did Rebecca see Philip Henry as a prosperous yeoman tenant farmer who could offer her financial security and a substantial house? Perhaps all these possibilities were part of the picture.

For Rebecca, a middle-aged woman used to making hats and living in a relatively urban environment, life as a farmer's wife at Towan with a family of nine children to look after must have been a challenge. Did Rebecca ever become the hardworking, competent farmer's wife that Jane had been? The family story which has been handed down says that Jane's

---

66 *Kelly's Directory for Cornwall 1873: St. Austell.* London: Kelly and Co., 1872, p.818.

children resented their stepmother, that Rebecca disliked the children, and that Philip Henry, tired of conflict at home, gave each of his children a gold sovereign and a new suit of clothes and told them to leave his house. Is this story true?

During the first half of the nineteenth century, the Cornish economy was relatively prosperous, but from the mid-1860s it faced several challenges. The copper mining industry collapsed in the face of international competition from countries such as Chile and the United States, where production costs were lower, while Cornish tin mining, after a brief period of revival in the 1870s, was also in decline. Then the pilchard industry, so long a mainstay of the economy, began to fail as the pilchard shoals, which had for so many years come inshore at the end of the summer, ceased to arrive.

Historically, the working population of Cornwall was accustomed to moving from one location to another to make a living – to find work if employment was scarce, or to find better working opportunities if pay at home did not compare to what could be earned elsewhere. The move may have been 'up country' to London, the north of England, Wales, or further afield. Opportunities for skilled Cornish miners became especially good as new mines were opened in many parts of the world; Philip Henry had himself gone to Australia as a young man and done well in the gold mines of Ballarat.

Towards the end of the nineteenth century, emigration was facilitated by improvements in rail and sea transport and by an ever-growing range of related services to help the emigrants on their way. These included newspapers that advertised the latest job opportunities and lists of ship sailings; railways that offered special rates on tickets and often worked with the shipping agents to offer a package deal on combined rail and sea fares; government officials who offered free and assisted passages to encourage emigration to the colonies of the British Empire where labour was needed; and local provisioners who could provide suitable food for the journey.

None of Philip Henry and Jane's children were directly involved in mining or fishing, but the multiple blows to the Cornish economy impacted on everyone living in Cornwall. Whatever family relations were like at Towan, and no matter how the children might have wished to find nearby employment away from the farm, local opportunities were limited. Even if the Hammer sons wanted to continue farming, Towan was leased, not owned outright, by Philip Henry, and so could not be handed down to them as part of their inheritance. So, as the Hammer sons and daughters reached maturity, they began to leave Cornwall. And if Philip Henry did send his children off with a gold sovereign and a new suit of clothes, it could have well have been as much in the spirit of 'this will help you start a new life' as 'take this and get out!'

Philip Henry's first-born, Henry, as we have seen, began his working life as a pupil teacher, possibly at the board school in St Austell or Mount Charles, but by the mid-1880s he had moved to Abergavenny in Monmouthshire, South Wales. Here he met and married Emily Maria Bigwood. In 1887 she gave birth to their first daughter, Ethel Millicent, and in 1888 to their first son, Reginald. By the early 1890s the family had moved to St Woolos near Newport and Henry was working as a commercial traveller. A few years later they moved to 25 Llanthewy Road in Newport, where a second son, Lawrence Henry, was born in 1895 and a second daughter, Dorothy Opie, in 1897. Henry was now working as a flour and corn agent and the family continued to live at Llanthewy Road for many years.

The second son, Will, left Towan at about the same time as his elder brother, Henry, but instead of moving north to Wales, he moved to Hackney, in the East End of London. During the second half of the nineteenth century Hackney's population was growing rapidly, largely as a result of the extension of the railway system into the area and the construction of several docking facilities, such as the Royal Group of Docks, to handle the trade in goods of Britain's vast empire. Other industries soon followed, new jobs were created, and a wave of immigrants began to arrive to take up the employment opportunities that were on offer. Hackney has historically been tolerant of accepting people from around the globe, and has long had a multiethnic population comprised of those seeking employment and those seeking religious and political freedom: in the late seventeenth century Huguenots fleeing religious persecution in France settled there; in the 1880s Jews fleeing the pogroms in Russia arrived; while from India and China came seamen who worked on British merchant ships. Many more came from Ireland and other parts of Britain, including Cornwall, and Will joined the throng.

Will managed to find work as a butcher, and through his stepmother, Rebecca, met Susie Ellen Smith, the second daughter of Rebecca's sister Susannah. Will and Susie were married at the Parish Church of St Andrew, Haverstock Hill, in Camden on 9 April 1887: Will was twenty-two and Susie twenty-four. They set up house at 96 Rendlesham Road in Hackney, where Susie, who was a certified elementary school teacher, gave birth to their daughter, Mabel Ellen, in 1888. A son, Vernon Montague, was born in 1892, followed by Norman William in 1898 and Clifford Leslie in 1906. A photograph of Will with his wife and two eldest children, Mabel and Vernon, outside 96 Rendlesham Road shows that Will, like his father Philip Henry before him, saw a family portrait as an opportunity to make a statement about his position in life: 'I now have a wife and children, a house and a horse-drawn carriage.'

Will with his wife Susie and children Mabel and Vernon
outside 96 Rendlesham Road, Hackney

The family later moved to nearby 29 Downs Road, where they would live for many years. Will was by this time a successful and respected master butcher, and Susie had retired from teaching to assist him in running his expanding business.

Both husband and wife took their civic responsibilities seriously. They were members of the Liberal Party and took a strong interest in local politics. Many from Cornwall supported the Liberal cause, and the ethos of the Liberal Party in many ways reflected the beliefs of Methodism which had been adopted by a large part of the Cornish population. As Philip Payton writes in the 2nd edition of *Cornwall: A History*:

> *In general, Cornish Methodism exhibited a strongly egalitarian strand, reflecting the potential for socio-economic mobility and the relative lack of class consciousness in nineteenth century Cornwall. Its theology, stressing concern for the needy and the equality of men before God, matched the political ideology of Cornish Liberalism. And just as Methodism had emerged as a significant element of new Cornishness, so Liberalism too was seen to be distinctly 'Cornish'.*[67]

None of Philip Henry's children were Methodists, but Will was certainly Cornish. He spoke with a strong Cornish accent, so much so that the 1901 census enumerator who interviewed Will heard him say his surname as 'Hummer', rather than 'Hammer', and recorded it as such.[68]

Will soon progressed within the Liberal Party hierarchy: he became a Liberal member of the Metropolitan Borough of Hackney Council, and in 1912 he was elected as Mayor of Hackney.

While Will continued to support the Liberal cause, there was growing opposition from the local Labour Party, which was beginning to find strong support as the principal alternative to the Conservative Party. One of the leading lights of the Hackney Labour Party was Herbert Morrison, who had developed an enthusiastic following and, in the 1920 election,

---

67 Payton, Philip. 'If You Haven't Been to Moonta'. In Payton, *Cornwall: A History*, 2nd ed. Fowey: Cornwall Editions, 2004, pp.211–212.

68 The National Archives of the UK. Public Record Office. *England Census 1901: Class RG13; Piece 211; Folio: 164; Page: 57.*

Will, Mayor of Hackney

Morrison was elected Mayor. This was the first of Morrison's successful forays into local government and, with a talent for political strategy, he was subsequently elected for a variety of influential local government positions, including membership of the London County Council in 1922. In 1923, Will was elected Mayor of Hackney for a second time, as Morrison, moving from the local to the national political arena, stood for election as the Labour Member of Parliament for South Hackney. He was elected and continued to rise within the Labour Party hierarchy: in 1929 he accepted his first Cabinet post, as Minister of Transport in the government of Labour Prime Minister Ramsay MacDonald.

Will's duties as Mayor were largely civic and ceremonial. In February 1924, during his second tenure, Will, along with his wife Susie, now an Alderman on Hackney Council, hosted a reception at Hackney Town Hall for Council members to meet the Lord Mayor of London, Colonel Sir Louis Arthur Newton and his wife. Invitation to the reception included participation in an At Home hosted a week later by Will and Susie. The reception was a grand affair, and guests danced foxtrots, waltzes, and one-steps to the Clay Dance Band throughout the evening. In addition, there

RECEPTION BY THE MAYOR AND MAYORESS in the Council Chamber from 7 to 8 p.m.

Reception of the Rt. Honourable the Lord Mayor, the Lady Mayoress and Sheriffs at 9.30 p.m.

During the Evening two Short Plays produced by Mrs. Henderson, will be performed.

At 8.15 p.m.
"THE LAST WISH"
(Written by Mr. Wm. Henderson.)
The Student ... ... W. Henderson.
The Soldier ... ... N. Atkins.
The Woman ... ... Kathleen Owen.
The Stranger ... ... Vernon M. Hammer.
Scene: A lonely cottage.
During this Play the Curtain will be lowered twice.

The time of second Play will be announced by the Master of Ceremonies during the Evening

"DICK'S SISTER."
Dick ... ... J. Dickinson.
The Lady ... ... Kathleen Owen.
Scene: Dick's Rooms.

DANCING.
The Dancing will be suspended during the Reception of the Rt. Hon. the Lord Mayor and His Lordship's Party, also during the Plays, if the Music is found to be inconvenient to the Players.

Master of Ceremonies:
Mr. H. Bloodworth, N.A.T.D.

PROGRAMME.
1. Fox Trot ... "Last Night on the Back Porch"
2. Valse ... "Wonderful One"
3. Fox Trot ... "Felix kept on Walking"
4. One Step ... "Sweetie"
5. Valse ... "Three o'clock in the Morning"
6. Fox Trot ... "Dancing Honeymoon"
7. Valse ... "Slave Song"
8. Fox Trot ... "Oom Pah"
9. One Step ... "Some-one"
10. Valse Cotillon ... "Blue Danube"
11. Fox Trot ... "Just keep on Dancing"
12. Valse ... "Dear Love"
13. One Step ... "I'm wild about wild men"
14. Fox Trot ... "You've got to see Mamma"
15. Valse ... "Nelly Kelly I love you"
16. One Step ... "Oh! Harold"
17. Fox Trot ... "Swinging down the Lane"
18. Valse ... "I'll sing thee Songs"
19. Fox Trot ... "Tin Soldiers"
20. One Step ... "They call it Dancing"
21. Valse Cotillon ... "Doctrinen"
22. Fox Trot ... "Every Day"
23. Valse ... "Kiss in the Dark"
24. Fox Trot ... "I love me"

Part of Will and Susie's invitation to their
reception for the Lord Mayor of London

were two dramatic presentations: *The Last Wish* and *Dick's Sister*, with Will and Susie's son Vernon acting the part of 'The Stranger' in *The Last Wish*.

Susie Hammer died in 1931 and, a year later, Will, aged sixty-seven, married Elizabeth Congdon Thomas, then thirty years old. The couple had a son, Harry Hammer, in 1935 and until Will's death, sometime between 1951 and 1958, the family continued to live at 29 Downs Road in Hackney.[69]

After Will, Kate was probably the next to leave Towan. Of all the children, Kate would have found it hardest to adjust to the arrival of Rebecca as her father's second wife. Since the death of her mother, she, as the eldest daughter, had taken on a lot of the responsibility for looking after the younger children and helping her father run Towan. She remained at Towan for a few years after her father's second marriage, but when she left she travelled about as far away from the farm and her

---

69 Will is listed in the Electoral Roll for South Hackney for 1951, along with his wife, but by 1958, she is listed in the Electoral Roll for Surrey as living with her son in Surbiton, Surrey, so Will died sometime between these two dates.

direct family as she could go: to Australia. Her uncle, Richard Hammer, had settled in Ballarat, Victoria, where her father had mined as a young man, and she might have chosen to join her relations there; but even this was not far enough. Having taken the long voyage to Australia, she then travelled on to Hobart, Tasmania.

As she was a single woman, her long outward-bound sea journey would not have been easy. An extract from a female emigrant's letter, written after a voyage out to New Zealand, advises what to bring and how to behave, and gives a good idea of the conditions Kate would have encountered:

My advice is to bring as few things as you can, luggage being one of the most troublesome things possible for single women ... you must have one box that you can get at once a month during the voyage. Into it put all your best things ... also a carpet bag with a good strong lock. In it put twelve shifts, to save washing, for if you have to wash with salt water, it spoils them ... also eight or ten pairs of stockings and two flannel petticoats, besides the one you have on, so that you may have enough to last the voyage ... as well as any work you could bring to do during the voyage – knitting or sewing, thread for tatting, or anything you can get. Bring a towel in your bag: you will find it very useful ... A large tin of biscuits would be a good thing to bring. Some brandy and a little ginger-wine is also good to have in case of feeling unwell from seasickness or other causes ...

Be frank, obliging and kind to all; but make a friend of no one and keep your tongue still, for there is always some scandal and bother going on ...

I forgot to tell you to have a hat on when you leave home, not too good to wear on board ship, and have some bits of stuff in your carpet bag to trim it up after a while, as it will soon look shabby. Also have a dress in your bag to wear on Sunday, with collar and cuffs. You must also have some light print frocks to wear in the tropics ... After that comes the cold, for which you must have worsted cuffs and a good warm jacket to wear all day; also a shawl or cloak to take around with you, for the cold is severe.

Above all, do not answer any letters that may be written to you by any of the sailors or passengers for, as they [sailors] are not allowed to speak, they write. You will go to church on board just the same as on land.[70]

When she arrived in Hobart, Kate found work as a housekeeper, a job at which, thanks to her years of practice at Towan following the death of her mother, she no doubt excelled. A photograph she sent back to her family from Hobart shows a serene, competent woman.

Kate in Tasmania

In 1913, whatever her experiences during the voyage out to Tasmania, she decided to make the return voyage to England to visit family and friends, and one young member of the Hammer family recalls that Kate's skin looked very brown and wrinkled for her age, perhaps the result of living in a climate so different from that of her native Cornwall.[71] After spending some nine months in England, early in 1914, Kate returned to Hobart, where she took up the post

---

70 Mayers, Lynne. 'You Will Find a Towel Very Useful: Extract from Chambers' Journal No. 551 (July 1874)'. *Cornwall Family History Society Journal.* (March 2012), p.33.
71 Conversation with Kate's niece Dora Hammer, the author's mother, who was a small girl when she met Kate on her return from Tasmania.

of housekeeper at Bishopscourt, in Fitzroy Place, the residence of the Bishop of Tasmania.[72]

If she had arrived at Bishopscourt a few years earlier she would have been able to try out her childminding skills on the young Bernard Montgomery, later to win fame in the Second World War as commander of the British Eighth Army: under his leadership, the Allies' victory at El Alamein marked a turning point in the Western Desert Campaign. His father was Bishop of Tasmania from 1881 to 1901, and Bernard was only two years old when the family arrived at Bishopscourt. His father was often absent – away in far-flung parts of Tasmania for months at a time – and his mother was strict and authoritarian, so Bernard enjoyed demonstrating his independent nature by challenging her and he remembered Bishopscourt as a place where *'One was hemmed in ... one was opposed ... one had to break out'*. According to his elder brother Donald, Bernard was always in trouble, and first gained his reputation as a rebel during his childhood in Hobart.[73]

Bishopscourt, the Bishop of Tasmania's residence,
where Kate was housekeeper

72   Bishopscourt is now known as the Old Bishop's Quarters and offers luxury vacation apartments for rental. Accessed 17 October 2020 https://www.bishopsquarters.com.au/.
73   *Monty – Old Bishop's Quarters*. Accessed 19 October 2020, https://www.bishopsquarters.com.au/monty-1.

On retirement, Kate continued to live in Hobart. She never married. Perhaps the experience of helping to bring up so many of the young Hammer children turned her away from any thoughts of marriage and children. She died in February 1932 and is buried in Cornelian Bay Cemetery in Hobart.

Next in age to Kate among the Hammer children was Philip. He is listed in the 1881 England census as living at Towan Farm,[74] but does not appear in the England census again until 1911.[75] Where did he go? There is a family story that says he went to Melbourne, Australia, and there became a jockey and, although there is no proof for this, horseracing was well-established in Melbourne, where a permanent racecourse was established in 1840, and horseracing was by the end of the nineteenth century a major industry, providing employment for trainers, jockeys, and stable hands. Whether Philip worked as a jockey in Melbourne or not, by 1907 he was back in Cornwall, and in July of that year he married Ellen Inch, known as Nellie. Ellen was born and had lived all her life on Porthpean Road, Mount Charles, St Austell, not far from Towan Farm. The couple settled in Mount Charles, and Philip worked with his father-in-law, John Inch, and his three sons as a cooper, making casks for the local china clay industry. Five years later Ellen gave birth to a daughter, Bertha Ellen Inch. The family stayed in the area for the rest of their lives, although they occasionally travelled further afield for a walking holiday: a photo of them taken in Ilfracombe, on the north coast of Devon, shows Philip and Nellie sensibly dressed and armed with walking sticks.

In later life Philip worked for a local marine dealership, where boats were built, bought, sold, and repaired. He died at his home in Mount Charles at the end of 1951.

After Philip came Annie, born in 1868. By the early 1890s she had left Towan and was living with her eldest brother Henry and his family at Goldfield House, St Woolos, in Wales. Here she found work as a draper's

---

74 The National Archives of the UK. Public Record Office. *England Census 1881: Class: RG11; Piece: 2302; Folio: 41; Page: 22.*

75 The National Archives of the UK. Public Record Office. *England Census 1911: Class: RG14; Piece: 13761; Schedule Number: 80.*

Philip and his wife Ellen

assistant, but by 1902 Annie was in Cape Town, South Africa, where, in November of that year, she married Alfred Charles Thurstans[76] – she was thirty-four, and he was twenty-six. The couple had no children, and later moved on to Hobart, Tasmania, from where in 1913 Annie sailed with her sister Kate to England, returning to Hobart in late 1913. Annie and her husband Alfred now lived, along with Kate, at Bishopscourt, where Alfred worked as an accountant. Perhaps it was Kate who helped Alfred find employment.

In 1916, Alfred – then forty years old – volunteered to fight in the First World War, joining the 40th Battalion Australian Infantry as a second lieutenant. Alfred was unfortunately killed in action during the Battle of the Ancre – the last phase of the First Battle of the Somme. He is buried at the Méricourt-l'Abbé Cemetery, in Picardy, France.

At the time of her husband's death, Annie was back in England, staying with her brother Ernest and his family in Hackney. When Ernest and his family left London for Essex, she moved nearby to her brother Will's house, but by late 1921 she was off again, this time to Melbourne.

---

76   South Africa. Parish Registers 1801–2004, Cape of Good Hope, Cape Town, St Barnabas Marriages 1898–1928. Marriage solemnized at Cape Town in the Division of the Cape, in the Parish of St Barnabas.

In 1935, aged sixty-four, she set sail one last time – from Sydney, New South Wales, Australia, bound for England and Cornwall. She went to live with her brother Charles and his family in Cornwall, where she stayed until her death in 1939.

Both Kate and Annie were born in the Victorian era, when a woman's role was clearly defined. It was believed that men and women had different characteristics and that women, although considered physically weaker, were morally stronger, and therefore best suited to the responsibilities of running the home and bringing up the children. This was one of the arguments against giving women the vote – that women, being fully occupied in the domestic sphere, did not have time to vote, or keep abreast of political developments, and therefore lacked the expertise to hold a useful opinion on political matters. Women in the United Kingdom would not get equal voting rights with men until 1928. So when Kate and Annie's mother died, they helped run the family home, gaining the kind of female expertise that was so admired by the Victorians.

Kate was able to make use of these skills to gain employment as a housekeeper in Tasmania, and established a settled and independent life for herself in Hobart, while Annie led a wandering existence which took her from Cornwall to Wales, and back and forth to South Africa, Australia, and Tasmania, until she finally returned to Cornwall. During her few years of married life, she had a house of her own, but otherwise depended on her brothers and sister to give her a home. Was she a free spirit who, once she had the money available, travelled where and when she wanted, but was happy to stay with family when funds were short? Was she happily married, and devastated by Alfred Thurstans' death, or did the relationship not work out? Was she a disappointed woman who married late, had no children, was widowed early and, unable to earn a living, was dependent on her siblings? She seems a quite different personality to her sister Kate, who made her way independently to Tasmania, settled there, and supported herself throughout her life.

Annie's younger brother Charles was only seven years old when his mother died, and he stayed on at Towan, helping on the farm until, in 1894, he married Beatrice Rowe, who was from nearby Polgooth.

Charles and his wife Beatrice

News that diamond deposits had been found in the British-owned Cape Colony of South Africa reached the newly-wedded couple – probably through the well-established information network that existed between Cornwall and the Cornish mining community in South Africa – and Charles and Beatrice decided to emigrate to the Eastern Cape, where Charles no doubt hoped to follow in his father's footsteps and make his fortune. South Africa was a popular destination for Cornish migrants, and in 1895 alone over 2,000 of them arrived, hoping for a better life. The family settled in Grahamstown,[77] established as a military outpost in 1812 by Lieutenant-Colonel John Graham, as part of Britain's effort to secure the eastern frontier of the Cape Colony on what had been Xhosa land. About 20,000 Xhosa had been forcibly pushed out to the lands that lay just to the east of the outpost, and Graham and his men had implemented a scorched earth policy, destroying Xhosa homes and crops to prevent them returning.

While Charles was in Grahamstown, his brother Fred was also in the Eastern Cape, and sister Annie was in Cape Town – about 600 miles (965 km) from Charles. Did they manage to meet? It is good to think that at some time they did and were able to catch up on all the family news.

---

77 The town's name was changed from Grahamstown to Makhanda in 2018.

Charles and Beatrice had their first daughter, Maud, in Grahamstown in 1896 but, not too long after their arrival, the already unstable relationship between the British and the Boers – descendants of earlier Dutch settlers – began to deteriorate. Between 1880 and 1881 the British and the Boers fought what is known as the First Anglo-Boer War, which ended with a British defeat and the British Prime Minister William Gladstone granting the Boers self-government of the Transvaal and the Orange Free State. Although defeated by the Boers, Britain was determined to expand its agricultural and mining interests in resource-rich South Africa, while the Boers, under the leadership of Paul Kruger, began to fear that the colonial policy of Joseph Chamberlain, then Secretary of State for the Colonies, would soon deprive the Boer Republics of their newly won independence. Kruger's government was further concerned by the high number of immigrant miners who flocked to the gold mines of the Witwatersrand and remitted much of their earnings to their home countries rather than spending it to benefit the local economy. About 25 per cent of the foreign mining work force was Cornish and, from the Transvaal alone, an estimated £1 million a year in remittances was being sent back to Cornwall. To cut down on the number of immigrants and recoup some of the money leaving the Boer Republics, Kruger decided to tax the immigrant miners while denying them voting rights. This move was unpopular both with the miners and with the British mine owners, and was one of many causes of the outbreak of the Second Anglo-Boer War. It also resulted in many Cornish miners leaving South Africa – Charles and his family among them. In October 1899, four months after they left South Africa, the Second Anglo-Boer War began, a conflict which ended in victory for the British and the return of the Transvaal and the Orange Free State to British control.

After a short stay in London, Charles and his family returned to Cornwall and settled on Black Acre Farm in St Columb Major, where a second daughter, Ivy, was born in 1900. Black Acre was a small farm with about 40 acres of black, peaty soil – hence its name – and Charles added to his income by working as a farm bailiff for one of the nearby large landowners, possibly the Duchy of Cornwall. The family later moved to a farm in Merry Meeting, a hamlet in the valley of the River Camel, near to the town of Bodmin. Here a third daughter, Phyllis Lilian, was born in April 1903.

While Charles was still helping on the farm at Towan, his younger brother Arthur was working as a grocer's assistant in St Austell. When Charles married and travelled to South Africa, Arthur also left Towan and moved to Newport, Monmouthshire, in Wales to join his eldest brother Henry. Here he met Sarah Vida Monckley, a West Country person like himself, born in Bideford, Devon. He married her in 1898 and began to earn his living as a commercial traveller selling shop fittings. Arthur and Vida set up home in Kenwick Van Road in Caerphilly, and here they had four children: Irene, Enid, Frederick, and Ruby.

Philip Henry's son Ernest was only three years old when his mother died. When he left school, he first worked on the farm at Towan and then tried life as a teacher until, in his early twenties, he moved to Hackney where he, like his elder brother Will, became a butcher. He lived at 54 Old Hill Street, Stamford Hill, and in 1902 married Harriet Morley who lived in nearby Mare Street. Harriet's family background was culturally diverse, and typical of many Hackney residents. Her Jewish great-grandfather, Edward Morley, had come from Holland, while her mother's family were descended from Swiss Quakers. Her parents, Samuel Morley and Harriet Farrow, had a Quaker wedding and afterwards settled in nearby Stoke Newington, not far from Hackney, where her father earned his living as a saddler and harness maker.[78] Shortly after their marriage, Ernest and Harriet moved down the road to 86 Old Hill Street, and there they began to add to their family: Vera was born in 1903, Frederick – known as Freddie – in the following year, and Dora in 1906. By now Ernest was, like his brother Will, a master butcher, and had built up a successful business employing four assistant butchers.

---

78 Oglesby, Edith Grace. *The Morleys and the Farrows*. Unpublished, nd. Hand-drawn family tree of the Morley, Farrow and Hammer families compiled by the sister of Harriet Hammer (née Morley).

Ernest, centre, in his butcher's shop, with his
children – left to right: Dora, Vera, and Freddie – and staff

He also took an interest in his local community and became a member
of the local council on behalf of the Liberal Party. Unlike his father and
brother Will, Ernest opted for a more conventional portrait when he had
a photograph taken of his family in the garden at Old Hill Street. They
are in their Sunday best, complete with a rather wilting aspidistra – that
favourite indoor plant of the era!

Freddie sadly died of meningitis in 1912, the same year that Harriet
gave birth to another son, Dudley, while Kathleen, their youngest child,
was born in 1915. A few years later the family moved from London to a
farm in Noak Hill, near Romford in Essex, which Ernest named Pentowan.

Left to right: Ernest, daughters Dora and Vera,
wife Harriet, and son Freddie

Here he returned to the farming life he had known in his youth, while Harriet began a catering enterprise called the Pentowan Farm Café.

Frederick George, known as Fred, was the youngest of Philip Henry and Jane's children. Only two years old when his mother died, Fred stayed at Towan until the early 1890s. He became a mining engineer, possibly studying at the Camborne School of Mines, which opened in 1888: he is not listed as a student, but as the early enrolment records are incomplete he may have attended their classes. Alternatively, he may have studied at one of the small art and science schools which offered part-time day or evening courses in engineering and mining at several locations in Cornwall, the nearest to Towan being at Redruth,[79] or he may have been taught informally by an experienced mining engineer.[80]

In 1895, Fred emigrated to the Cape Colony of South Africa, perhaps encouraged by his brother Charles who was then living with his family in Grahamstown, in the Eastern Cape. Fred married his cousin, Lilian Alethea Hammer, daughter of his father's brother Charles Henry Hammer and wife Elizabeth, and in 1897 Lilian, accompanied by her young brother Harold, sailed out to Cape Town to join Fred. Two years later, Fred and Lilian had a son, who they named Hartley Charles Hammer.

Fred set up business as an engineer and worked on a contract basis throughout the region. In August 1903 he was employed by the owner of Erin Farm, which lies near the town of Middelburg[81] in the Karoo of the Eastern Cape, to open up an underground water source stored behind an ironstone dyke on the property.[82] The Karoo is a vast semi-arid region where the rainfall is low, and successful farming in the area depends on access to underground water. Fred set a dynamite charge to break open

---

79 Emails from Carole Green, Archives and Special Collections at Falmouth University, dated 16 and 18 September 2020.

80 Correspondence via Messenger with the St Austell Old Cornwall Society dated 24 September 2020.

81 Message from Kathy Anstiss concerning Frederick George Hammer's official Death Notice, sent via Messenger, dated 14 September 2020.

82 Ironstone is also known as dolerite and is extremely hard. The Karoo dolerite dykes were formed during the early Jurassic Period, over 200 million years ago. They are formed when molten magma flows upward through a near-vertical crack in an existing layer of rock and solidifies underground.

the dyke, but the fuse did not ignite. He unwisely went to inspect it, and the dynamite exploded, killing him instantly. Although Fred did not live to see it, the explosion succeeded in breaking the dyke, and a deep pit measuring 49 feet (15 m) by 82 feet (25 m) was dug to hold the water – enough to irrigate about 25 acres (10 ha) of land.[83]

Fred's brother Ernest named his first son, born a year after Fred's death, Frederick George, adding Albert as a third name, in memory of a brother who died so suddenly only a few months short of his twenty-eighth birthday.

After all his children had left Towan, Philip Henry continued to live on the farm with his second wife Rebecca; and his son Will, married to Rebecca's niece Susie, was a frequent visitor.

Left to right: Philip Henry, Will, and Susie at Towan

When he spent time with his father at Towan, Will – although now a Londoner – still enjoyed country pursuits, and in this photo Philip Henry, Will and their dog are about to go shooting.

---

83 Email to the author from Andrew van Lingen, the current owner of Erin Farm, dated 10 September 2020.

Will, Philip Henry, and their dog

Will, as in his mayoral photo, sits upright and a little stiffly as he looks straight at the camera, while his father looks far more relaxed and confident, ready to get on with shooting some game for the Towan kitchen.

Philip Henry and Jane brought up nine children, which was not an unusual number for the time, and they took care of Philip Henry's parents who lived with them at the Charlestown Mill, but the next generation of Hammers all had fewer children: Ernest and Harriet had five; Henry and Emily, Will and Susie, and Arthur and Sarah had four apiece; Charles and Beatrice had three; and Philip and Nellie, and Fred and Lilian had only one. Times were changing: families were smaller, and the small nuclear family was replacing the extended family that traditionally sheltered several generations under the same roof; while many families who had lived in the same village for generations split up, as younger members left home in search of employment and a better life.

Philip Henry's second wife Rebecca died at Towan in September 1898. She was sixty-five years old and had been married to Philip Henry for fifteen years. Seven months after the death of his second wife, Philip Henry married for a third time.

5

A Third Wife

Philip Henry married Emily Jane Adams in April 1899 at Holy Trinity Parish Church in St Austell, the church where he had earlier married Rebecca. Philip Henry was sixty-five, Emily was twenty-nine. Emily, the daughter of an agricultural labourer called John Brokenshire and his wife Jane James, had been born into a large family in Tresean, a small hamlet just north of the village of Cubert.

In January 1891 Emily had married Henry Adams, a farmer living at Harris Mill, Illogan, near Redruth. At the time of her marriage Emily was twenty-one. Henry was sixty-eight, and this was his second marriage: as a young man he had married Jane Trezona, but the couple had no children and Jane had died in 1888. Henry passed away only a year after his marriage to Emily and, still childless, left Emily a considerable sum of money. At only twenty-two years of age, Emily was a wealthy widow.

If the England and Wales Register for 1939 is correct, Philip Henry had taken more than a passing interest in Emily while Rebecca was still alive because, in May 1898, a few months before Rebecca's death, Emily gave birth to Philip Henry's son, John Edgar.[84]

Around this time, Philip Henry left Towan. Perhaps the lease had run out again but, at well over sixty years of age, he was no doubt ready to retire from farming and lead a less demanding life; and perhaps the lease on the farm was about to run out. With Emily, their son, and their

---

84 The National Archives of the UK. Public Record Office. *England and Wales Register 1939: Reference: RG 101/6695F.*

daughter, Violet May, born in 1899, he moved to a house in Fistral, St Columb Minor, near Newquay.

Will continued to visit his father, even though family relations between the two may well have suffered as Philip Henry's relationship with Emily blossomed while Rebecca, his second wife, and the aunt of Will's wife Susie, still lived at Towan. A photo taken of Philip Henry at Roche Rock shows the old man still determined to be photographed in a grand setting, even though he is no longer the tenant farmer of 140 acres. He is driving an open carriage, the horse's head held by the ever-obliging Will.

Philip Henry and Will at Roche Rock

Roche Rock is an imposing pinnacle of granite situated at the northern edge of the St Austell Downs, not too far from Philip Henry's new home at Fistral. *Roche* is a Norman French word meaning simply 'rock' and Roche Rock has long been a significant local religious centre. A medieval chapel was built on top of the Rock with a room below, in which, according to tradition, there once lived a hermit. The chapel window can be seen in the photograph at the top of the pinnacle.

By 1903, Philip Henry, Emily and their young family moved to a house in Church Row, Lanner, near Redruth, and here, on 24 May 1904, Philip Henry died. He was sixty-nine years old. Emily was now thirty-five and, three years later she married John Samuel Chapman, a farm labourer and cattleman, then aged forty-one. Samuel adopted the two children Emily had borne with Philip Henry, and in 1909 Emily presented Samuel with a daughter, Emily Jane.

During Philip Henry's lifetime Cornwall saw many changes. In his father John's day, the Cornish economy had depended largely on mining and fishing: copper and tin were in great demand, while pilchards were a staple of the local diet, and salted pilchards were a dependable export. But when ore was discovered in other parts of the world and proved to be cheaper to extract there, and when the shoals of pilchards failed to arrive off the coast, the narrow-based local economy began to falter, and Cornish men, and some women, began to look beyond the county for employment. Hard-rock mining skills were much in demand wherever ore was found in the world, and as a young man Philip Henry became part of the now growing Great Migration. In Ballarat he made his fortune as a miner and returned to Cornwall with the financial means to set up a business. By the time his children with his first wife, Jane, were of age, the local economy was growing steadily worse and, possibly partly motivated by a need to get away from their stepmother, they too joined the growing numbers of Cornish migrants.

Towards the end of Philip Henry's life there was a change in the nature of migration. With networks well established between the Cornish at home and the Cornish overseas, there were fewer families – like Charles and Beatrice, or Fred and Lilian – emigrating as permanent colonists. Instead, there was a new focus on itinerant workers who had up-to-date information on the best current work opportunities and who moved wherever a skilled deep-rock miner was needed, often returning to Cornwall before leaving again for a mining destination in a different part of the world. While this in the short term helped solve the unemployment problem and enabled the miners to send funds back home to their families, in the long run it encouraged a culture of dependency on remittances, so different from the prosperous independent local mining economy of earlier days:

Thus the prospect of Cornwall in the early 1900s, dependent so pathetically on the diligence of her exiles in distant South Africa, was as far removed as it could be from that of the vibrant assertive, innovative society that had existed less than a century before.[85]

As the Cornish economy continued to decline, most of Philip Henry and Jane's children continued to make lives for themselves away from Cornwall, but family members always returned to Towan. Will continued to visit neighbours in the Towan area until the 1950s, and later generations of the family went to look at the old house during summer holidays spent in Cornwall, often when it stood empty and untenanted. No matter how many generations removed from Philip Henry and Jane and how far from Cornwall they live, Towan will always be a place with memories for the Hammer family and their descendants:

Towan … Meadow, 2 acres; pasture, 3 leagues long and 1 league wide; woodland, one half league long and 3 furlongs wide.[86]

Five of the Hammer brothers back at Towan;
back row, left to right: Arthur, Ernest, Charles;
front row, left to right: Philip and Will

85   Payton, Philip, 'If you Haven't Been to Moonta'. In Payton, *Cornwall: A History*, 2nd edn. Fowey: Cornwall Editions, 2004, pp.235–236.

86   Storey, Tony. 'The Sawle Family of Penrice, Cornwall'. Accessed 19 October 2020, <http://www.sole.org.uk/sole2/penrice.htm>. (Originally published in the April 2002 edition of *Soul Search*, the journal of the Sole Society.)

Bibliography

Bainbridge, C. George. *The Wooden Ships and the Iron Men*. Charlestown: Charlestown Estates, 1980.

Balchin, W.G.V. *The Cornish Landscape*. rev. ed. London: Hodder and Stoughton, 1983.

Bennett, Alan. *Cornwall throughout the mid 19th Century*. Southampton: Kingfisher Railway Productions, 1987.

Benney, D.E. *An Introduction to Cornish Watermills*. Truro: Bradford Barton, 1972.

Borlase, William. *Observations on the Antiquities, Historical and Monumental, of the County of Cornwall*. Oxford: W. Jackson, 1745.

Broadhurst, Paul. *Secret Shrines: in Search of the Old Holy Wells of Cornwall*. Launceston: Broadhurst, 1988.

Buckley, Allen. *Cornish Bal Maidens*. Redruth: Tor Mark, 2010.

Buckley, Allen. *The Story of Mining in Cornwall*. 2nd ed. Fowey: Cornwall Editions, 2007.

Carveth, Richard. *St Austell Tithe Map and Apportionment 1841*. n.p.: 1848.

Chesher, V.M. and F. J. Chesher. *The Cornishman's House: an Introduction to the History of Traditional Domestic Architecture in Cornwall*. Truro: D. Bradford Barton Ltd, 1968.

Cope, Phil. *Holy Wells: Cornwall; a Photographic Journey*. Bridgend: Seren, 2010.

Cornwall Family History Society, 'Monumental Inscriptions Database'. Accessed 17 October 2020, http://www.cornwallfhs.com/.

Cornwall Records Office. 'Graham and Graham, Solicitors, St. Austell'. Documents Relating to the Estate of Samuel Moss of Boscundle, St. Austell.

Cornwall Records Office. 'Graham and Graham Solicitors, St. Austell. Lease, Charlestown, St. Austell, 1 January 1832'.

Courtney, M.A. *Cornish Feasts and Folklore*. Wakefield: EP Publishing, 1973.

Deacon, Bernard. 'A Forgotten Immigration Stream: the Cornish movement to England and Wales in the 19th century', *Cornish Studies* 17 (2009). Exeter: University of Exeter Press, pp.17–33.

Deacon, Bernard. *Cornwall and the Cornish*. Penzance: Alison Hodge Publishers, 2010.

Deacon, Bernard. *The Cornish Family: the Roots of our Future*. Fowey: Cornwall Editions, 2002.

Deacon, Bernard. *The Surnames of Cornwall*. Redruth: CoSERG, 2019.

French, Mary. *A Victorian Village: a Record of the Parish of Quethiock in Cornwall*. Falmouth: Glasney Press, 1977.

Geevor Tin Mine Museum. *Vocabulary of Cornish Mining Terms*. Penzance: Geevor Tin Mine Museum, 2009.

German Miners and Cumbrian Peat Carriers. Accessed 17 October 2020, https://thewildpeak.wordpress.com/2013/04/28/german-miners-and-cumbrian-peat-carriers/.

Guthrie, A. *Cornwall in the Age of Steam*. Padstow: Abby House, 1994.

Holmes, Julyan. *1000 Cornish Place Names Explained*. St. Agnes: Truran, 1998.

Jacob, Valerie. *St Austell through Time*. Stroud: Amberley Publishing, 2009.

Jenkin, A.K. Hamilton. *Cornwall and its People, being a New Impression of the Composite Work including: Cornish Seafarers, 1932; Cornwall and the Cornish, 1933; Cornish Homes and Customs, 1934*. London: David and Charles, 1945.

Kelly's Directory for Cornwall 1873: St. Austell. London: Kelly & Co., 1872.

Lane-Davies, Rev. A. *Holy Wells of Cornwall: a Guide*. n.p.: Federation of Old Cornwall Societies, 1970.

Larn, Richard and Bridget Larn. *Charlestown*. 2nd ed. Redruth: Tor Mark, 2006.

Larn, Richard and Bridget Larn. *Charlestown: the History of a Cornish Port*. Charlestown: Larn, 1994.

Last name Hammer. Accessed 17 October 2020, https://www.surnamedb.com/Surname/Hammer.

Leggat, P.O. and D.V. Leggat. *The Healing Wells: Cornish Cults and Customs*. Redruth: Dyllansow Truran, 1987.

Martin, Edith. *Cornish Recipes Ancient and Modern*. Truro: Cornwall Federation of Women's Institutes, 1929.

Maurier, Daphne du. *Vanishing Cornwall*. London: Virago Press, 2007.

Mayers, Lynne. 'You Will Find a Towel Very Useful: Extract from Chambers' Journal No. 551 (July 1874)'. *Cornwall Family History Society Journal*. (March 2012), p.33.

Messenger, Michael John. *Caradon and Looe: the Canal, Railways and Mines; the History of the Liskeard and Looe Union Canal, the Liskeard and Caradon Railway, the Liskeard and Looe Railway, and the Mines and Industries they Served*. Truro: Twelveheads Press, 1978.

Meyrick, J. *Holy Wells: a Pilgrim's Guide to the Holy Wells of Cornwall and their Saints*. Falmouth: Meyrick, 1982.

Monty – Old Bishop's Quarters. Accessed 19 October 2020, https://www.bishopsquarters. com.au/monty-1.

Nankervis, Jean. *Wicca: a Ffarm in West Cornwall; 6000 Years of History*. rev. ed. Zennor: Nankervis, 1991.

Noall, Cyril. *The Story of Cornwall's Ports and Harbours*. Truro: Tor Mark Press, 1970.

Oglesby, Edith Grace. *The Morleys and the Farrows*. Unpublished, n.d. Hand-drawn family tree of the Morley, Farrow and Hammer families compiled by the sister of Harriet Hammer (née Morley).

Parish of St Paul's Church, Charlestown, Cornwall. Accessed 17 October 2020, https:// www.stpaulscharlestown.co.uk/a-history-of-charlestown-parish-and-st-paul-s- church/.

Payton, Philip. *Cornwall: a History*. 2nd ed. Fowey: Cornwall Editions, 2004.

Payton, Philip. *The Cornish Overseas: a History of Cornwall's 'Great Migration'*. Fowey: Cornwall Editions, 2005.

Preston-Jones, Ann. *Towan Holy Well, St. Austell, Cornwall: Recording and Repointing*. Truro: Historic Environment Service, Environment and Heritage, Cornwall County Council, November 2006.

Quiller-Couch, Mabel and Lillian Quiller-Couch. *Ancient and Holy Wells of Cornwall*. London: Charles J. Clark, 1894.

Rule, John. *Cornish Cases: Essays in Eighteenth and Nineteenth Century History*. Southampton: Clio Publishing, 2006.

St Austell Feast Week. Accessed 17 October 2020, https://www.cornwallforever.co.uk/year/st-austell-feast-week.

St Austell Parish Genealogy. 'Charlestown Marriages 1860–1862'. Transcribed by J. Mosman, Online Parish Clerk, for the St Austell History & Genealogy website. Accessed 17 October 2020, http://freepages.genealogy.rootsweb.ancestry.com/~staustell/Structure/Genealogy.htm#mar.

St Paul's Church Congregation. *St. Paul's, Charlestown: a Parish Portrait with Historical Notes on Charlestown, Carlyon Bay, Duporth, Mount Charles, Holmbush, Boscundle and Par Moor.* Charlestown: Parish of St. Paul's, 2001.

Shipwreck and Heritage Centre. *The Story of Charlestown.* Charlestown: Shipwreck and Heritage Centre, n.d.

'St Austell. The Guardians', *Royal Cornwall Gazette*, Saturday 27 March 1875, p.6.

Stanes, Robin. *Old Farming Days: Life on the Land in Devon and Cornwall.* Tiverton: Halsgrove, 2005.

Stevens, James. *A Cornish Farmer's Diary: Selections from the Diary of James Stevens of Zennor and Sancreed (1847–1918)* edited by P.A.S. Poole. Penzance: Poole, 1977.

Storey, Tony. 'The Sawle Family of Penrice, Cornwall'. Accessed 19 October 2020, http://www.sole.org.uk/sole2/penrice.htm. (Originally published in the April 2002 edition of *Soul Search*, the journal of the Sole Society.)

Straffon, Cheryl. *Fentynyow Kernow: in Search of Cornwall's Holy Wells.* 2nd ed. Penzance: Meyn Mamvro Publications, 2005.

The National Archives of the UK. Public Record Office. *England and Wales Register 1939: Reference: RG 101/6695F.*

The National Archives of the UK. Public Record Office. *England Census 1881: Class: RG11; Piece: 2302; Folio: 41; Page: 22.*

The National Archives of the UK. Public Record Office. *England Census 1901: Class RG13; Piece 211; Folio: 164; Page: 59.*

The National Archives of the UK. Public Record Office. *England Census 1901: Class: RG13; Piece: 2207; Folio: 27; Page: 45.*

The National Archives of the UK. Public Record Office. *England Census 1911: Class: RG14; Piece: 13761; Schedule Number: 80.*

Thomas, Elizabeth. *Reminiscences of Mrs. Elizabeth Thomas 1817–1898.* n.p.: nd.

Whetter, James. *The Cornish Farmer: a Study of a Parish and a Family.* Gorran: Lyfrow Trelyspen, 2001.

Index